Hope for a Change

By the same author

From India with Hope
Experiment with Untruth
A Different Accent
On History's Coattails

HOPE
FOR A CHANGE

*Commentaries
by an
Optimistic Realist*

MICHAEL HENDERSON

GROSVENOR BOOKS

Copyright © 1991 by Michael Henderson

Published by
Grosvenor Books
3735 Cherry Avenue, N.E.
Salem, OR 97303

Also available from Grosvenor Books at:

54 Lyford Road
London SW18 3JJ
England

21 Dorcas Street
South Melbourne, Victoria 3205
Australia

Suite 405, 251 Bank Street
Ottawa, Ontario, K2P 1X3
Canada

PO Box 1834
Wellington
New Zealand

Library of Congress Card Number 91-073157

British Library Cataloguing in Publication Data

Henderson, Michael, *1932-*
   Hope for a change: commentaries by an optimistic realist.
   I. Title
   909.829

ISBN 1-85239-507-9

Cover design: Susan Applegate of Publishers Book Works, Inc.
Cover photo: Jerome Hart

Typeset in Sabon by Irish Setter, Portland, Oregon
Printed by Edwards Brothers of Ann Arbor, Michigan

TO
Gerald & Judith

Contents

Introduction

IN THE SUMMER of 1943, at the height of World War II, I was a very small and very proud English boy in a large crowd of mostly uniformed American soldiers. We were listening to British Prime Minister Winston Churchill in Harvard Yard. He had just been awarded an honorary doctorate of laws and his speech underlined the importance of post-war Anglo-American cooperation and of American leadership.

He said on that occasion:

> If the people of the United States had remained in a mediocre station, struggling with the wilderness, absorbed in their own affairs and a factor of no consequence in the movement of the world, they might have remained forgotten and undisturbed beyond their protecting oceans. But one cannot rise to be in many ways the leading community in the civilized world without being involved in its problems, without being convulsed by its agonies and inspired by its causes. If this has been proved in the past, as it has been, it will become indisputable in the future. The people of the United States cannot escape world responsibility.

1

The passing of the years has not diminished the validity of Churchill's words. Indeed, the ending of the cold war and the attendant problems have only given them new content.

I was present that day because I was one of thousands of young British children who were given refuge by American families at a time when it looked as if our country would be invaded. The arrival on these shores of my brother, Gerald, 6, and me, 8, in August 1940 was marked by a front-page photo in the *Christian Science Monitor*. The caption said of my brother as we lined up for the immigration inspection, "Gerald's impression of the proceedings seems a bit questionable." He had his tongue stuck out at the photographer.

Our impressions of this country, however, have never been questionable. They have always been marked by gratitude, the kind of gratitude shared by millions around the world who have known first-hand American hospitality and generosity.

After working in many parts of the world, my wife, Erica, and I, with our daughter, Juliet, have come to live in the United States. I am, officially, a resident alien, which sounds a little like a cross between E.T. and "Our man in Portland." It means, in practice, that if we behave ourselves we can stay indefinitely.

We came here after Watergate and Vietnam, to use the shorthand for events that have tormented the American soul. But we have lived through Contragate, Irangate, the savings and loan scandals, the Gulf War, doubts about America's competitiveness, and all.

Celebrations to mark the ending of the cold war and the demolishing of the Berlin Wall gave way swiftly to dismay both at the emergence of old hatreds which had been kept in check and at the cost of restoring dilapidated economies. Euphoria at the decisive win in the hot war in the Gulf was followed rapidly by concern at the plight of the Kurds and frustration with the difficulties of wider peace-making in the Middle East. Soon U.S. troops were helping in Bangladesh. People find themselves on a roller-coaster of emotions.

As I travel the country I meet Americans who look for reassurance and above all hope. The structure of the media and particularly news reporting practices do little to respond to that need. The news reinforces in many people a sense of powerlessness. Some people tell me, almost with satisfaction that they have given up watching television or have canceled their newspaper subscriptions.

Editors make great efforts these days to produce papers that are reader friendly, as the phrase goes, a product you don't want to leave home without. That is why they create shopping mall and freeway beats, use color graphics, provide handy news summaries. But sometimes they neglect to include that ingredient of hope and vision that prepares people to tackle immense problems or even to cope with daily living.

I have been fortunate over these years in the United States and in other countries to have had the chance not only to meet people whose convictions and actions encourage hope, but also to talk about them on the radio. The commentaries in this book were all broadcast either on the stations of Oregon Public Broadcasting (KOPB, KOAC, KOAB, KRBM) or on KBOO Portland and KMUN Astoria.

They are in some cases about people who could easily regard themselves as victims but who have triumphed over adversity; people whose decisions to get involved have taken them into positions of responsibility they neither sought nor expected; people who do not have "blame" in their vocabulary. Some are part of a global fellowship of people of all backgrounds who take faith seriously and try to live the way they want their countries to live. It goes by the name Moral Re-Armament, or simply MRA.

We are entering what futurist Robert Theobald calls the rapids of change. There's not much calm water around. Learning how to protect the lives of spotted owls and the livelihood of forest workers, how to maintain any kind of world order and yet respect the rights of people to go it alone if they choose;

how to preserve privacy in the midst of an unparalleled information revolution, and many other issues, some as yet unthought of, will tax human imagination, and ingenuity and spirit. As we equip ourselves for what could be a bumpy ride we will need generous doses of hope and reassurance.

The problems, the agonies, the causes, touched on by Churchill, are with us to stay. Too many people around the world depend economically and to an extent spiritually on the wellbeing of the United States for it to falter at this time. This book is a contribution to a balance of outlook and a growth in character and stature that could be indispensable for American leadership.

1 A changing world

IN 1843 THE U.S. COMMISSIONER of patents claimed that the advancement of the arts from year to year taxes our credulity and "seems to presage the arrival of that period when human improvement must end."

In 1885 the U.S. commissioner of labor forecast that the day of large profits was probably past. "There may be room for further intensive, but not extensive development of industry in the present era of civilization," he said.

In 1989 the deputy director of the State Department's policy planning staff announced that we were witnessing "the end point of mankind's ideological evolution." Borrowing the vocabulary of Hegel and Marx, Francis Fukuyama wrote, "It may be the end of history."

Beyond the cold war

THE 1990S ARE A GIFT to the people of Eastern Europe, and, God willing, the hour of freedom will strike in this decade for the people of South Africa and China and other countries that have not yet benefited from the wave of democracy.

Enormous problems in Eastern Europe and insecurity in the world at large may follow, but it is a blessing that these can be confronted within a freer framework. In the East leaders and populace will need forgiveness, patience, vision, and that largeness of spirit exemplified by Czech President Vaclav Havel's "We are all to blame."

But the 1990s are also a gift to the United States. They offer the chance to break out of the cold war box that has encased all of us more than we realize.

For years millions hailed communism as the answer while millions saw it as the problem. Clichés and stereotypes still hold sway on both sides.

Without the cold war would we have had the spectacle of a House Un-American Activities Committee? Without the cold war would we have been dehumanized to the point of justifying the moral correctness of the threat to use nuclear weapons? Without the cold war and the resulting hot wars would we have a society and a culture that is so addicted to violence? Without the cold war might not America have made spectacular progress in helping feed, clothe, and house the world?

Oregon's senior senator, Mark O. Hatfield, believes that what he calls "the distorting lenses of superpower rivalry" has always shortchanged American initiatives. He has called for refocusing attention on a new agenda—global reconciliation. He says instead of military competition both superpowers must carry their wars to the front lines of such issues as global poverty, and America must move beyond containment to "a prudent partnership" that can strengthen practical cooperation between developed and developing nations. In an essay in *Christianity Today*, he writes, "Only by remaining true to the values that made America free, can she expect to stay free, because the core of those values represents the common aspirations of all mankind." He believes that a United States with new priorities "could again capture the world's imagination."

Superpower cooperation has already shown results in Southern Africa, Central America, and Eastern Europe. And whether or not that cooperation continues, perhaps the greatest "peace dividend" for the United States will be a new freedom of thinking and acting in global affairs.

More than a hundred years ago the great Russian writer Dostoevski described a nation's mission as: the belief in one's desire and ability to give the world a message, and to renew it with the abundance of one's vitality; a belief in the sanctity of one's ideals; and a belief in the strength of one's love and yearning to serve mankind. These beliefs, he said, were the pledge of a nation's highest existence and the one means to endow succeeding generations with vitality. "Only a nation strong in this belief," he wrote, "has the right to a higher life."

It would be nice to hope that we can replace the arms race with a race to see who can more fully and more quickly live up to Dostoevski's challenge. The United States has a head start there. And I don't expect a bear to catch an eagle, but then I don't forget that the tortoise once passed the hare.

19 JUNE 1990

Ticket to Budapest

FOR HIS CLARITY on the sins of atheistic materialism Alexander Solzhenitsyn was hailed in this country. But for his temerity in pointing out the sins of Western materialism he was then relegated to the u.s. media's back burner. The heroes now are the new leaders in Eastern Europe, but how long will they remain so if they start drawing attention to weaknesses in our society that they do not wish to import? How long will they remain heroes when they start challenging our way of life?

The Reverend Laszlo Tokes, who helped spark the Romanian uprising, explains that what is happening in the East "is not just a political revolution but a religious renaissance." Secretary of State James Baker asks, "Could it be that a major meaning of the revolution going on in Eastern Europe is the resurgence of faith?"

For decades many Western liberal intellectuals have fostered the view that religion, if not a lie, was at least irrelevant to matters of nationhood. Now we have Eastern intellectuals, like President Havel of Czechoslovakia, talking naturally of faith as a factor in their lives and in the affairs of state.

Cardinal Franz Koenig, the former archbishop of Vienna, as much as anyone in the West, played a vital part in encouraging the changes in Eastern Europe. Thirty years ago, at the prompting of Pope John XXIII, he began his visits through the Iron Curtain. It was at one of his first audiences that Pope John asked him to see Cardinal Mindszenty in exile at the U.S. embassy in Budapest. Koenig thought it would be difficult. "What's so difficult about it?" said the Pope in his direct way. "Walk to the station in Vienna, buy yourself a ticket to Budapest and simply go there."

Cardinal Koenig reminds us that communism in Eastern Europe has been a relatively recent phenomenon, whereas Christianity came to those countries a thousand years ago. Those roots, he feels, need to be nourished. There must be new economic arrangements and generous terms given to these "emerging" nations. But we need, above all, rather than foisting on them our militantly consumerist society, to help them rediscover their finest traditions and qualities. Setting people free to choose, he maintains, is not only the freedom of the market but the freedom to choose between God and Mammon. As Pope John Paul said in Czechoslovakia, to avoid new disasters the building blocks must be forged with spiritual, moral, and cultural values.

Newsweek columnist Meg Greenfield points out that we have plenty to learn from those who have struggled heroically against oppression. "It will be our disaster and, in its way, Stalin's revenge," she believes, "if we take the thrilling turn of events in the world as evidence that we have perfected our own society and are unflaggingly faithful to our own principles."

An English doctor, John Lester, has returned from Poland with the conviction that if we are humble enough to learn, people there have much to teach us. He says a new era is being built by those who have not compromised, by those who refused to cooperate with the "lie." He suggests that perhaps we in the Western democracies need to measure ourselves on the same scale. We may not have had to face governments committed to untruth. And yet at every level of society it is easier to compromise for the sake of an easier life, for the sake of promotion, or to be thought well of, than to hold to standards that we know to be true and unchanging.

This is quite a challenge. Could that be part of what Lech Walesa is looking for when he says, "We look to America and expect from you a spiritual richness to meet the aspirations of the twentieth century."

1 MAY 1990

Christ and the Kremlin

DR. BRYAN HAMLIN, a friend in Cambridge, spoke last month in the Harvard University Chapel about his recent visit to the Soviet Union. In the plane he read a copy of *Moscow News* in which a senior Politburo advisor was calling for the Soviet Union to repent for the massacre of Polish officers at Katyn toward the end of World War II. So in Moscow Hamlin found the senior Politburo advisor and they had a fascinating conversation. The Russian told Bryan that he had come to the conclusion that Marxism did not fit with the realities of human nature and was an antithesis to Christianity. To Bryan's amazement he said, "I'm reading the Bible. I read a passage from the Bible and then something from Karl Marx and compare the two. Marx doesn't come out too well in comparison."

The December issue of *Moscow News* carried the results of a public opinion poll done by the Soviet Academy of Sciences. The final question: "Which of the following names will, in your opinion, be of great importance to the people of the USSR in the year 2000?" Forty-eight percent felt that Andrei Sakharov would still be of importance; 26 percent felt that about Gorbachev. But 58 percent said they believed Jesus Christ would be of the greatest importance to the people of the Soviet Union a decade from now. This in a land where for more than 70 years the authorities have tried to suppress Christian faith.

Extraordinary stories are coming out of the Soviet Union: the respectful manner in which Soviet generals received a gift of Bibles from the Gideons, the response to Portland evangelist Luis Palau, the fact that Mikhail Gorbachev is the son of a God-fearing Russian Orthodox mother and almost certainly himself baptized, the springing up of 3000 new Orthodox parishes in the first half of 1989 compared with three in the whole of 1985, and Christmas celebrated in Red Square with tree lighting and cathedral bells heralding Jesus' birth and the Soviet Navy band playing "Silent Night."

For a comprehensive survey of the changes and a caution about their significance, I recommend the superb book *Gorbachev, Glasnost and the Gospel* by Michael Bourdeaux, one of the most respected and consistently accurate observers of the religious scene in the Soviet Union.

Many years ago American journalist John McCook Roots had an encounter that is worth thinking about now. In his biography of Chou En-lai, Roots describes meetings with Mikhail Borodin, the Soviet agent who did more than any other foreigner to communize China and later was a founder of *Moscow News*. "I was sitting, notebook on knee," Roots writes, "questioning him with the unconscious arrogance of the privileged young Westerner amid the squalor of the East." They got to talking about missionaries.

"After a long silence," Roots goes on, "Borodin, still gazing out the window, began murmuring half to himself. 'You know,' he mused, 'I used to read the New Testament. Again and again I read it. It is the most wonderful story ever told. That man Paul. He was a real revolutionary. I take my hat off to him!' He made a symbolic gesture, his long black hair falling momentarily over his face. Another long silence. Then suddenly Borodin whirled, his face contorted with fury as he shook his fist in my face. 'But where do you find him today?' he shouted. 'Answer me that, Mr. Roots. Where do you find him? Where? Where? Where?' Then furiously, triumphantly: 'You can't answer me.'"

Borodin's passionate outburst recalls Lenin's words, recorded in *Letters on Modern Atheism*, "I made a mistake. Without doubt, an oppressed multitude had to be liberated. But our method only provoked further oppressions and atrocious massacres. My living nightmare is to find myself lost in an ocean red with the blood of innumerable victims. It is too late now to alter the past, but what was needed to save Russia was ten Francises of Assisi."

As masses of Christians of all stripes flood into the Soviet Union with their often conflicting messages, it may be good to remember that it is the life and commitment of Christians that will appeal to those people. They have had enough of dogma.

It may be good also to consider that the people of the Soviet

Union who have been faithful under persecution may have more to teach us than we realize. As the *Christian Science Monitor* wrote last year, "The West has seen the East bloc in terms of what it needs—freedom, wealth. Yet the West can also learn much from the spirit of religion exhibited in the East —a profound seriousness that's willing to put all on the line."

Let me end with another curious angle. Karl Marx did his high school thesis on St. John's Gospel. In a letter to a friend he wrote, "When all the political foundations of religion are wiped out, when the organization and the institutional structure of the church are destroyed, then normally religious faith, the Christian faith, would have to disappear. But it is not out of the question that the Christian faith will survive anyhow. This would mean that there is a religious reality that does not depend solely on the sociological and the institutional; under these conditions, we would have to heed this reality."

This is a Marxist analysis I would go along with. It's a pity we had to wait so long for the reality to be recognized.

14 MARCH 1991

Berlin's revenge

IF THERE IS historical irony, it is surely what I have just encountered in Berlin. The few sentences that have appeared in news agency reports hardly do justice to what must be a unique development.

Most older Americans will remember the dramatic days of the Berlin airlift. On the night of June 23, 1948, when the Soviet military administration cut off the city's electricity and disrupted all road and rail traffic between Berlin and the Western occupied zones, U.S. General Lucius D. Clay ordered in planes to supply the inhabitants. Over the next 11 months

200,000 flights brought in 2 million tons of food, clothing, fuel, and industrial goods. Eighty-four Americans, British, and Germans lost their lives in this difficult operation. The $200 million cost was borne by American and British taxpayers.

To ensure that the city would never again be vulnerable to blockade, an emergency stockpile was set up—food for 6 months, industrial supplies for 3. Along Berlin's inland waterway, in warehouses and silos, a vast storehouse has been maintained, regularly restocked and inspected.

And now the whole lot—500 million marks worth—is being handed over gratis to the very people who have made life difficult for the Berliners for 40 years—the Russians. The list of the official "reserves," as they are called, includes everything from 66,000 tons of rye, 26,000 tons of canned beef, 21,000 tons of canned vegetables, 19,900 tons of sugar, and 12,200 tons of skim-milk powder to 3250 tons of toilet paper, 2000 tons of washing-up liquid and 269 tons of matches.

Parallel to this government action is the massive private giving to the Soviet people by the German people. Everywhere I went in Germany, in hotels, in government offices, and in stores, I saw boxes, containers, jars marked "Help Russia." Newspapers and TV and radio have mounted huge campaigns. Just as Americans after World War II sent Care packages to Europe, now Germans are doing the same to the Soviet Union.

Much of this, no doubt, is a thank you to Soviet President Gorbachev who made reunification possible. Some of it may be, as has been suggested, an unconscious affirmation of superiority, or a desire by Germans to show that the past is at last truly put behind them. But to a visitor this wave of spontaneous outpouring to others, despite problems at home, is an impressive show of generosity to a people in need and, certainly for the Berliners, a desire to share with others the kind of solidarity from which they have benefited over the years. "Once you have needed it," Eckhard Stratenschulte of the Berlin mayor's office told me, "you know how important it is. The Americans helped us, now we will help the Russians."

26 DECEMBER 1990

Romanian roadblock

IT WAS LIKE a scene from a spy thriller. Just before midnight on Christmas Day 1990 on a cold freeway 60 miles west of Bucharest the car was stopped by a roadblock and surrounded by fifty armed men, some in uniform, some not, who threatened the passengers. But it was for real—and frightening.

King Michael of Romania, accompanied by Queen Anne and other members of the royal family, was on his way to pray at the tombs of his ancestors at Curtea de Arges. It was the exiled king's first visit to his country in 43 years.

The 69-year-old monarch is no stranger to conflict—or to the fight for freedom. In 1944 he led a coup against the pro-Nazi government and brought his country into the war on the side of the Allies. In 1947 he was confronted in the palace by the communist prime minister who told him that several thousand students would be killed if he refused to abdicate. "I could not take responsibility for a bloodbath," said King Michael. Four days later he left the country.

With the apparent changes in Romania he has wanted to revisit his country. In April 1990, however, the Romanian government prevented his making a private Easter visit, claiming that it was too close to the elections. Later, the authorities said that they had withdrawn their objections.

On Christmas Day, in a Swiss chartered jet, on a flight route previously approved by the Romanian civil authorities and guided by Romanian air traffic control, the royal party landed at Romania's Otopeni airport. After an hour's wait their passports were stamped and approved. As they were leaving the airport they were asked to return their passports as the authorities, it was claimed, had omitted to transcribe certain details. Some of the party remained behind to deal with the matter.

So the roadblock came as a great shock. Under threat, the party was escorted back to the airport and, after long negotiations in which, according to National Public Radio correspondent Kate Hunt, the king behaved "with incredible dignity," the royal party was put on a Romanian plane and flown back to Switzerland. During the whole time they were prevented from having any communications with the government, with embassies, and with the king's eldest daughter, Princess Margarita, who was in Bucharest. They were not even allowed to depart in the plane in which they had come because, according to the authorities, the pilots were incapacitated by drink.

The royal press office said that this new obstruction by the Romanian authorities could not deflect the monarch from his "immutable wish to travel to and in Romania as a free citizen of the country, without any restrictions and preconditions."

The Romanian government called the visit "clandestine," a "cheap sensation," and "totally illegal," and accused the airport authorities of a "weak reaction." The interior minister conceded that the police had displayed a "lack of professionalism." Opposition parties condemned the expulsion.

US News and World Report expects that there will soon be a military coup in Romania and that the country will revert to a constitutional monarchy. Although the king has wide backing from intellectuals, support for him could hardly be described yet as popular. After all, for 40 years he has not only been a non-person but history has been rewritten to the extent that young Romanians I have met have even been told, incorrectly as part of disinformation, that he cannot speak Romanian.

If the present rulers continue to treat him and the country in such a cavalier fashion, there must surely be an increased appeal for a man who can be, in his own words, "a national leader who can unify the country and help the will of the people to be expressed in freedom and democracy."

3 JANUARY 1991

The Munich syndrome

I SAW THE MOVIE *Dances with Wolves* the other night. A magnificent film but I didn't enjoy it. Not with war going on in the Middle East. One is more powerfully reminded of the reality, cruelty, and senselessness of war in one cinema evening than in hours of censor-cleared, military-sanitized versions of the war in Iraq and Kuwait, courtesy of CNN.

This is not an argument for more blood to match the thunder, nor a criticism of the powers-that-be, but simply a statement that this film destroys any illusions about the nobility of war.

I happened to phone a congressional office just before the Gulf War started. I began to ask a question and was told, "Sorry I haven't time to talk. Are you for or against the war?" I understand that reaction from a staff member who was inundated by calls that day and anxious to tabulate the public mood. But it was a misleading over-simplification.

Those who resist the idea of going to war are sincere. The men of Munich have been ridiculed ad nauseam for having appeased Hitler. But think what those men had lived through in World War I, only 20 years earlier.

My father served as a private in the trenches in France. On only the first day of the 1916 battle of the Somme about the same number of British soldiers were killed as were Americans in the entire Vietnam War. It was 15 times the later British losses on D-Day, 7 times the losses at the battle of Waterloo.

Eleven hundred alumni from my old school, Mill Hill (whose enrolment at that time varied between 150 and 265), were in the services. A small illustration to think about in the context of your own high school football team: all fifteen members of the school's 1913 rugby team were in the forces overseas and eight of the team were killed.

The men of Munich knew what they were trying to prevent. Hindsight, and probably wisdom, says that they were wrong to appease. It seems indisputable that if Hitler's appetite for other people's countries had been resisted earlier the second World War might have been prevented.

I don't know whether it is right to characterize Saddam Hussein as another Hitler. His track record of starting wars, invading territory, and gassing his own people would suggest that it is. I don't know whether better diplomacy, greater restraint, and more patience would have got him out of Kuwait. No one knows. And, without excusing Saddam Hussein, we need to admit the Western shortcomings over more than 50 years in that part of the world, that have fed instability and resentment.

War always represents a failure of peaceful means to resolve conflict. But some wars have to be fought. And sometimes sooner is better than later. Certain issues transcend life or survival. It is why we honor those who lay down their lives for others. And why asking whether you would want to send your own son or daughter to war is not the fundamental question. This war has brought together the international community in rare unanimity in support of United Nations' objectives. At this stage one can only hope and pray for a rapid victory.

I spoke on the phone this week with an Egyptian-born American. He naturally feels the situation very deeply. His wife is Argentinian. Yet another war has invaded their living rooms. "We will win the war," he said with assurance. "But we will lose the peace."

I hope he is right on the first prediction and wrong on the second. Assuming we win—and win quickly—the world at large will have to weigh the gains of removing a military threat to the nations of the Middle East (and the possible control an unscrupulous man might have been able to exert on the world's energy supplies) against the resulting poisoned relations between Muslim and Christian nations. A strengthened and more united United Nations will have to be set against the bitterness and desire for revenge in millions of hearts.

So far America's public statements, by both military and civilian leaders, have been restrained. General Schwarzkopf ("Norman of Arabia" as one English journalist has called him) is very familiar with the issues in the Middle East and President Bush has a genuine desire to see the United States be a healing influence in a post-war world. But it will not be difficult for Saddam Hussein to be portrayed by some as a hero standing up to a bullying West.

Dr. Charis Waddy, an expert on the Middle East who is author of *The Muslim Mind*, spoke wise words at the publication party for her book in London: "One thing is certain. Next week, next month, next year, the issues that confront mankind will still be there: poverty, starvation, disease, debt, and the enmities, deprivations, the cruelty and greed in wounded hearts that perpetuate these problems. Whatever the outcome in the Gulf, war will not cure them. Today or tomorrow, they have to be addressed, intelligently, drastically, lovingly. Who is ready to build now?"

31 JANUARY 1991

A way for the Kurds

IF HITLER had not gone to war what would have been the legal basis for foreign nations to intervene to save the Jews? The question comes to mind when one sees the backs and forths of aid to the Kurds of Iraq and the hums and has of how to receive the Dalai Lama in Washington, D.C. When can governments forget legal niceties, as Mrs. Thatcher called them, and let hearts dictate rather than diplomatic calculations? Whom do you help? Those covered by TV news? We obviously can't help everyone.

It is not an easy matter. But some ground seems to have been broken in the latest concept of safe havens for the Kurds, put forward by British Prime Minister John Major and adopted by European and U.S. governments.

World peace and security depend on certain international conventions, principally the sanctity of borders. It is why the Organization of African Unity froze the borders of Africa despite the fact that they were arbitrarily drawn by European nations. This is in a large measure what the Gulf war was about. It is why India, for instance, while accepting the recent U.N. resolution establishing the formal cease-fire between Iraq and the U.S.-led coalition, expressed reservations on provisions that might be interpreted as giving the U.N. Security Council a role in imposing boundaries between nations.

Article 2.7 of the U.N. charter says, "Nothing contained in the present Charter shall authorize the United Nations to intervene in matters which are essentially within the domestic jurisdiction of any state."

A former British ambassador, Archie Mackenzie, who was at the founding of the United Nations in San Francisco in 1945, remembers well the feelings about sovereign rights and the smaller countries' fears of interference by greater powers. It was they, he says, who favored this article. The word "essentially" was inserted in it so that it should not unduly limit U.N. action and become a cloak for chicanery.

Yet what does "essentially" mean, he asks. Does it mean exclusively? And what is exclusively the concern of only one country in the shrunken world of the 1990s? Very little, he replies. The denial of human rights in Burma? Or in the Baltic countries? Or human rights for the Kurds? Or in Northern

Ireland? Is drought in the Sahara merely a domestic problem? Or a nuclear accident in the Ukraine?

In the magazine *For A Change* Ambassador Mackenzie writes, "The U.N. has been trying to adjust to the dramatic changes in the world's structure since 1945, but much too slowly. It now needs active support from all of us so that our governments do not hide behind Article 2.7 when inconvenient issues arise; so that problems get dealt with in their infancy, before they have grown into mind-boggling disasters; and so that the same standards are applied to all. We need not so much to change the Charter as heighten our commitment to it. Could this be our response to the sacrifices in the Gulf?"

British Foreign Secretary Douglas Hurd says in support of Prime Minister Major's initiative: "It would be perverse if international rules, put in place to make the world safer, were to oblige us to turn a blind eye to inhumanity. That is why we have taken a lead in pushing forward the boundaries of international practice. Our approach is concerned with people rather than territory. Safe havens do not have to be precisely defined by boundaries. The refugees cannot afford to wait for stately discussion."

It must now be hoped that the United Nations or the International Red Cross will swiftly replace the United States in safeguarding the lives of Kurds.

23 APRIL 1991

Canada's place

CANADA DAY CELEBRATIONS were somewhat muted in our northern neighbor following the breakdown of the Meech Lake Agreement, which was designed to resolve the country's constitutional difficulties. In fact, in Quebec City and some other French-speaking towns the official observance of Canada's equivalent of the Fourth of July was cancelled. "We have no business celebrating a country that slams its door shut on our fingers," said Quebec City Mayor Jean-Paul L'Allier.

One hopes that wiser sentiments prevail in the long run as Canada has so much to celebrate. And surely no Canadian can look with equanimity at a possible break-up of the country, with Quebec's deciding to opt for independence, and some provinces even trying to become u.s. states.

Peter Jennings, the Canadian who is ABC's anchor, cannot conceive of Canada without Quebec any more than he can a United States without California, Louisiana, or Ohio. How right he is. The great debate north of the border has been all about the "distinct society" of Quebec. Perhaps the result would have been more fruitful if there had been more debate about "the distinct society" of Canada.

The Queen of England, who is also Queen of Canada, was in the dominion last week. In a rare intervention in political affairs she seized the chance to plead for national unity. "It is my fondest wish for this Canada Day," she said, "that Canadians come together, rather than dwelling on the differences which might further divide them.

"I am not a fair-weather friend," she told a crowd on Ottawa's Parliament Hill, "and I am glad to be here at this sensitive time. There is in Canada, and about Canadians, a constant search for fairness, a receptiveness to honorable accommodation, enabling the two principal language communities to flourish within the Canadian family. Those values are needed now more than ever." The Queen said that the summer months should provide a time of "calm reflection" and rethinking.

In a world where more and more ethnic groupings seem to want to go it alone, Canada has been an inspiring example of people of different backgrounds getting it together—native Americans, French speakers, English speakers, other ethnic groups, and, more recently, Chinese. Canada has played a leading role in the Commonwealth, in Francophonie (the association of French-speaking countries), and in the group of leading industrial nations, the only country to belong to all three significant world groupings.

Dr. Vivian Morris Rakoff, a leading Canadian psychiatrist, is concerned about the way Canada, in its current constitutional crisis, seems to be shooting itself in the foot. He told journalist Peter Newman of *Maclean's* magazine, "Here we are, one of the world's happy countries, not perfect but essentially benign, welcoming and decent. We've absorbed millions of immigrants and haven't cracked apart, and while there have been some terrible racial incidents we have had no race riots. We are at peace and perpetuate no major international quarrels. We are the seventh most prosperous country in the world and share our wealth higgledy-piggledy across the country. And yet we seem to be tearing ourselves apart as though we were a Lithuania that was annexed without legality, as though we were oppressed by some offensive, powerful, outside regime. It's madness. Why are there people who want to break this country apart? It's like being given one of God's great gifts, deciding it may not be totally perfect, and breaking it to see what's inside."

On my last visit to Canada it was hard at times to realize that the country might be on the verge of dissolution. For most people it seemed to be business as usual. There was an apathy. Indeed, many friends of Canada living abroad have been astonished how calmly many Canadians, at least outwardly, are taking the threat of a break-up of the country. Perhaps it is because they somehow know it is not going to happen, or perhaps it's because they fear it will break up and feel they can do nothing about it.

Peter Jennings, comparing what is happening in Canada with what might happen in the United States if it were in a similar situation, wrote in *Maclean's*, "It would simply not be possible in the United States for eleven politicians to be sitting around a table negotiating the breakup of their country without millions of Americans publicly demonstrating their refusal to accept this outrage."

On an earlier trip to Canada I was given a copy of the official *Canada Handbook*, which states, "Canada is the third largest country in the world in terms of land area." Pasted inside the front cover was an erratum slip, "Page 29, first line of paragraph 1 should read "Canada is the second largest country." An innocent error, but in some ways also a reminder that Canadians are quick to forget their place in the world.

5 JULY 1990

Who's destroying the planet?

"THERE ARE too many people on our planet. Too many children being born. Look at the problems it causes everywhere." This is the kind of thing one hears said without contradiction. Yes, but one might well ask, where are these "too many" people? You're not talking about my daughter surely, or your son? Where are these "too many" people? In the third world, you say. Ah, you mean somebody else's son or daughter.

So this obvious fact of overpopulation we like to talk about involves somebody else's changing their way of life.

Why should they? Ah, they're just selfish, you maintain. Look at the way all those third world countries are ruining the world's precious life support system. Remember that *Time* magazine cover story. Its map, which must now be on thousands of walls in this and other countries, gives overpopulation as one of the greatest threats to the earth's environment. The accompanying text states, "The world's population, now at 5 billion, is increasing at least 80 million every year. About 90 percent of the growth is occurring in developing countries, where most people struggle to eke out an existence. The swelling tide of humanity is wreaking havoc on the environment by chopping down forests, overgrazing grasslands, and over-plowing croplands in a desperate effort to produce more food."

There it is, all those third worlders who can't stop having babies and are threatening our future. Sounds pretty convincing. But, wait a moment didn't I read an article in the *National Geographic* that had a rather different perspective? It was a major piece by Paul and Anne Ehrlich of the Department of Biological Sciences at Stanford University, in which they said that the birth of a baby in the United States "imposes more than a hundred times the stress on the world's resources and environment as a birth in, say, Bangladesh. Their lifestyles," they wrote, "do not require huge quantities of minerals and energy, nor do their activities seriously undermine the life-support capability of the entire planet."

Concerned about the discrepancy between these two statements in *Time* and the *National Geographic*, I contacted the Ehrlichs at Stanford and found that they, too, were disturbed by the misleading summary in *Time*. In fact, they sent a letter to the magazine (which was not published) in which they drew the important distinction that while population problems in poor nations are major factors in keeping them poor, population problems in rich nations are destroying the ability of earth to support civilization.

I have no wish to minimize the problems that will accrue as we add to the earth the equivalent in population of a new North America every three years. Increased food production and improved distribution alone will not suffice. I would only make the plea that we in the West maintain an appropriate humility in our approach to those who live in less-developed societies; that when we prescribe remedies that may offend ancient ways and even religious traditions, requiring others to change, we remember who is doing the most to destroy the ecosystem we all depend on. Or, put another way, let our motivation be not: slow the growth so that we can continue to enjoy a life style of conspicuous consumption and waste, but rather: let us work effectively together to give a decent life to every single inhabitant on this earth, their children as well as ours.

7 MARCH 1989

2 American originals

To SUGGEST THAT Patrick Henry may never have actually said, "Give me liberty or give me death," would get me into trouble in Virginia. But, in fact, his words were only reconstructed 40 years later. To say that Lincoln's famous ten points, like "You cannot bring about prosperity by discouraging thrift," were formulated by someone else, may disillusion some. But in truth there is no evidence to connect them with any known Lincoln writing or statement. And to state that Vince Lombardi never said, "Winning isn't everything, it's the only thing," is to repeat what the coach himself confirmed.

For this and other disconcerting news I am indebted to an entertaining new book *Respectfully Quoted*, a dictionary of quotations from the Congressional Research Service, published to celebrate the two hundredth anniversary of the founding of the legislature. As the book's editors say, "There are a surprisingly large number of Americanisms which never passed the lips of those to whom they are attributed." Or as Will Rogers might have put it, "The trouble with people is not that they don't know but that they know so much that ain't so." Only Rogers probably never said that either, nor did Josh Billings.

Hurt and hopeful

GENERAL COLIN POWELL can be described as "the most powerful black man in the world," according to an article in Britain's daily *The Guardian*. "He is a living refutation of the glib slogans about America as an incorrigibly racist society," writes Martin Walker, "and by all accounts an exceedingly fine and decent man."

So it was curious to me that Chairman Powell of the Joint Chiefs of Staff was not even mentioned in a syndicated article this past week by Coretta Scott King, in which she reviewed blacks' historic contributions to the u.s. armed services.

But then, sadly, the war and particularly the large numbers of black u.s. troops in the Gulf has become a contentious issue in the black community. Though constituting only 12 percent of the American population, they make up 25 percent of the troops in the Gulf area.

I am aware how strongly some black friends feel about this issue. They know personally, they say, young blacks who signed up just to get out of poverty.

But it seems to me that for some black leaders this disproportion is just a stick with which to belabor political opponents or to bolster an anti-war stance. For after all, more whites than blacks must have joined up for that same reason. Research shows that the blacks in the armed forces are generally better educated and from more affluent families than their white counterparts. And the only way to prevent the higher number of blacks entering the services would be to establish a quota system or to institute the draft.

The *New York Times* quotes Professor Charles Moskos, a military sociologist at Northwestern University, who says, "The military is the only major institution in America with something like a level playing field. It is the only place where a white will be bossed around by a black on a regular basis at the local level. There is probably a better racial climate in the military than on a college campus."

General Powell, the twenty-six black generals, and the black troops in today's U.S. military inherit a long tradition of service and of courage, some of it not recognized until years later. More than 5000 blacks served in the Revolutionary War, for instance, but, as Coretta King points out, it was not until 1986 that an act of Congress authorized a memorial to them in Washington, D.C.

On Powell's Pentagon office wall is a picture of Lieutenant Henry Flipper, the first black to attend West Point. He was hounded out of the army after a trumped-up embezzlement charge in 1881 and only exonerated in 1979. He commanded the Buffalo Soldiers who helped win the West. Powell led the campaign to have a monument built to these soldiers.

The 6-foot-1-inch, 200 pound-plus soldier grew up in the South Bronx, the son of Jamaican immigrants, his father a shipping clerk, his mother a seamstress. "There was an expectation that you were supposed to do better," he remembers. "The key to opportunity in this country begins with education. My parents expected it. Children watch the way their parents live their lives. If they like what they see, they will live their lives that way too. If the parents' values seem correct and relevant, the children will follow those values."

General Powell entered the army not through West Point but through the Reserve Officer Training Corps at the City College of New York. He served with distinction in Vietnam and later as national security adviser.

He told David Wallechinsky in a *Parade* magazine interview that for more than 300 years blacks had fought for this country in the military in times of danger, and during most of that time were only allowed to serve when there was dying to be done. It has been in the last 30 years, in his generation, that full integration and opportunity had been achieved. "But blacks have never turned that into a condemnation of society," he

says, "never lost their love of country. As much as I have been
disappointed in my lifetime that we didn't move as fast as we
might have, or that we still have forms of institutional racism,
we have an abiding faith in this country. Hurt? Yes. Losing
faith or confidence in the nation? No."

General Powell is well aware of the criticism that in the Gulf
War the undue burden falls on blacks. But he points out that
before the war began the criticism reaching him was that op-
portunities in the military were shrinking for blacks just as
blacks were using it as a stepping stone for advancement.

As a foreigner I would be sorry to see political issues deflect
attention from the tremendous contribution of black Americans to this United Nations-approved effort. I think we have
much for which to thank them.

Historically blacks have done better after wars. And no war
before the present one has so depended on their participation.
This Gulf War could hardly have proceeded without them.
Coretta King says, as I mentioned, that "delayed appreciation
of black veterans has been a common denominator of every
American war." So, in so far as it is right to single out service
by race, I suggest we can thank the black soldiers best this time
by making sure that the war on the home front to eradicate
poverty and prejudice is prosecuted with the professionalism,
modern means, and adequate funding that has characterized
the Gulf War.

21 FEBRUARY 1991

Julie's story

I MISSED a plane connection the other day at Chicago's
O'Hare airport and, thanks to the airline, had the chance to
hear a fascinating story. There were just three of us in the
shuttle to the hotel at which the airline was putting me. "Are

you going to the conference?" the driver asked me. It turned out that 125 legislators from around the country were meeting at a conference organized by Americans United for Life.

Well, we got talking about abortion and pretty soon I made one of those remarks one makes about disliking the polarization, and though I was against abortion, I thought I would make exceptions in the case of rape or incest.

"You don't know who you're talking to, do you?" said the only other passenger, a vivacious women, who for all I knew might have been a beauty queen. Of course not, I thought, we hadn't been introduced. But there was something in her tone of voice that made me realize that wasn't what she meant.

Julie Makimaa, as a young married woman in Michigan, knew that she had been adopted and wanted to find out who her real parents were. For 4 years she searched. A number pencilled lightly on the margin of her adoption papers turned out to be the key. It was the telephone number of a friend of her natural mother. If Julie had phoned a few weeks later the number would have been disconnected. It transpired that Julie's mother, Lee, like Julie, was a devout Christian, as were their respective husbands, and Julie's adoptive parents. Lee believed that one day God's radar, as she called it, would lead her child back to her again. After talking on the phone they agreed to meet.

Then came the hard part. Julie had to be told that she was the result of a rape. Lee's husband encouraged her. "You need to make it clear that you are not the type of girl who was just sleeping around and got caught." In fact, Lee had been an 18-year-old virgin who was taken advantage of at an "office party." With the help of Christian friends she had decided to have the baby, although she never saw the child because she was delivered under anesthesia and immediately the baby was turned over to an adoption agency. Lee was too poor to care for her child.

When Julie heard the news there was no emotional stress,

just intense gratitude that she had been born. "I was very sorry that my mother had to go through that terrible experience," she says, "but I am so thankful that I am here. For me, I feel that it doesn't matter how I got here, what's important is what I do now." Julie's husband's first words to Lee were, "I want to thank you for not aborting Julie. I don't know what my life would be without her and my daughter."

Julie told me she had started an organization called Fortress to defend women who become pregnant and children conceived through sexual assault. She believes society has treated women as if they were criminals, by doubting their honesty and accusing them of causing the assault, and by treating the resulting children as if they were to blame by giving them the death penalty.

Lee has written a book, *The Missing Piece*, describing what she has been through. Opening the book I notice a note to me from Julie, "Hope our story will be encouraging to you. God is big enough to handle the 'hard cases.'"

It certainly is encouraging. And I'll be more thoughtful about what I say in airport buses in future.

25 SEPTEMBER 1990

A straight arrow

NORMAN ORNSTEIN, resident scholar at the American Enterprise Institute, believes that individual members of Congress are cleaner, more sensitive to ethical lapses and conflicts of interest, and more resistant to corruption than at any time in our history. He says they are largely people who are trying to do what is best for their districts and country, working harder than those in most professions, and not in the job to make a fast buck or simply for power and acclaim. According to *The*

Economist, "Personal venality is not Congress' problem, except in isolated and quickly discovered instances. Its rules are tougher than those that affect lawmakers in most countries."

This is not the usual image of our members of Congress because of the ethical lapses of some and because of issues like pay raises. Nor is the fuss over ethics a new phenomenon. Mark Twain called members of Congress the only "distinctly American criminal class."

"He wouldn't accept toothpaste if he were sharing a room with me." This is how a friend of mine jokingly describes the incorruptibility of a certain lawmaker. If Ornstein is right he may not be unique but I would like to tell you about him.

Charles E. Bennett, for 41 years a Democratic representative from Florida, is regarded as the father of ethics legislation in the House, although he does not feel that you can legislate moral fiber. In 1967 he introduced the bill that created the House Ethics Committee, now called the Committee on Standards of Official Conduct, and was its first chairman. Interestingly, he voted against the recent ethics legislation, even though many of its provisions are based on bills he introduced earlier, because it was tied to a 40 percent pay raise by 1991. He would only agree to a raise, he says, if it were tied to a cost-of-living index and was not retroactive. He believes he is already adequately paid and that the benefit of public life "is the joy of doing something worthwhile, the chance to serve your fellow man."

Bennett is a stickler on financial matters. For instance, he regularly returns to the treasury the disability pension he receives for polio contracted during service in the Philippines in World War II, and has never spent more than $30,000 in an election campaign.

There is one area in which the recent ethics bill did not go far enough to satisfy him: it did not stop members who are seeking election to leadership positions from passing on campaign contributions to other members. Jack Anderson, in one of his columns last fall, pointed out that one representative had doled out $60,000 from his reelection fund to other House Democrats to line up support for and secure the chairmanship of the Armed Services Committee. His opponent, Charles Bennett, refused to give any money.

The Florida Representative would also like to see a Constitutional amendment to limit the amount of money spent on political campaigns, and ways found to reduce the enormous sums needed for television campaigning, which can make legislators prey to the influence of political action committees.

Since 1951 Bennett has not missed a single legislative vote— he has answered to over 16,000 recorded votes and roll calls. He takes the practice of his Christian faith just as seriously. It was he who introduced "In God we trust" as the national motto.

Last summer, in the face of what it called the Great Ethics Frenzy gripping the House of Representatives, *US News and World Report* asked two savvy capitol hill insiders to list veteran representatives whose integrity was beyond question and then to pare the list down to the dozen straightest arrows. One name on the list was Charlie Bennett.

23 JANUARY 1990

Donna Rice post mortem

SHE CAME. She saw. She fled. That could sum up the story of Donna Rice's non-speech to the national convention of the Society of Professional Journalists (SPJ) in Cincinnati in November 1988. But it would only be part of the story.

The model and actress, whose liaison with former U.S. Senator Gary Hart ended his bid for the presidency, had been invited to speak at the convention on the subject of the invasion of privacy. Her flight from the cameras before she even entered the hall provoked considerable soul-searching on the part of the disappointed journalists. "We learned more about sensitivity to privacy than we would have if she had shown up," said Oren Campbell, a delegate from Oregon.

It wasn't journalism's finest half hour, even in a simple matter like accuracy: the *Cincinnati Post* described how 800 SPJ members were waiting as "about twenty photographers and reporters" ran toward her as she approached the meeting. The *Cincinnati Enquirer* said 700 were waiting as Rice swept past "about eight" photographers and journalists. It was left to the editor of the *Enquirer* to do a Dewey-over-Truman. A column that appeared two days after the incident, and tried to convey the impression that it was written at the end of the convention, informed readers that the session in which "Donna Rice talked about the Gary Hart affair" was one of those that "drew the largest crowds and the most outside interest."

At an extra meeting specially squeezed into an already tight program, society members debated the significance of what happened and who was to blame. Some felt that Donna Rice had intended to snub them all along. "None of us were convinced it was not planned from the beginning," said Beverly White, morning news anchor of WKRC-TV in Cincinnati. "If you're allergic to animals you don't go to the zoo." Others contended that Donna had genuinely wanted to share what she had learned. "I don't think we were being had," said James Plante, outgoing president of the society. "She wanted to talk. She could have given us some valuable insights into privacy." Some journalists castigated the behavior of some of the working press for going beyond what was acceptable in pursuit of a story. Others faulted the society's officers for not easing Donna's entry into the hall.

As a first-timer at such a gathering of American journalists, I was struck by the degree of rethinking going on by many, though by no means all, in the profession. Perhaps the strongest speech, given on the opening day before the Donna Rice affair, was by William Burleigh, senior vice president of Scripps Howard. He said that instead of calling journalists to arms on behalf of the First Amendment he wanted to challenge those present to examine the flip side of the amendment—responsibility. He named some specific needs of journalism—to be accurate and fair, credible and balanced; to explain itself better to society and respond to its critics; and to protect freedoms outside its narrow range of interests. He also attacked arrogance as a disease that was "gnawing at our innards."

Burleigh said that forty editors and other prominent newspeople, who had been the subject of news stories themselves had been interviewed earlier this year in the *Los Angeles Times*. They had harsh things to say about inaccuracies, preconceived story lines, and a seeming indifference to or ignorance of basic fundamentals of news gathering and journalistic ethics. "When the arrow strikes so close to home," he told us, "we can hardly pass off the criticism as misguided or ill-informed or issued from a poisoned source."

No matter how well the press was doing, even if, as some felt, we were the best ever and the world's best, it wasn't good enough, he said. We were being called to a higher standard. Because much of the public didn't trust and didn't believe the press.

This widespread concern, raised by Burleigh, was mirrored in the professional development seminars at the convention, with subjects like ethics and the future direction of news. Incoming president Paul Davis said he would make journalistic ethics a main focus of his year in office. Christian Anderson, editor of the *Orange County Register*, warned that the future of newspapers was at stake, with leisure time at an all time high and yet the public's choosing not to read newspapers.

It was clear, from the youthfulness of many of the delegates and the awards to student chapters, that the Society of Professional Journalists puts much emphasis on the training of young journalists. Whether these young men and women would have been reassured by their experiences at the convention that they had chosen the right career, I do not know. But I think the public would certainly have been encouraged by the convention's preoccupation with improving the service which the media provide.

I hope we may yet hear from Donna Rice. She says she still wants an opportunity to share her experiences. Perhaps the society will be better prepared next time. Though it can't say of every member, as was said of Sam Donaldson at a roast marking his retirement from the White House beat, "He has promised to be a kinder, gentler correspondent."

1 DECEMBER 1988

A son set free

SOMETIMES A PHRASE jumps out at you from a book. It illuminates a truth or opens up an avenue of thought in a way volumes before have not done. Sometimes a scene in a film cannot be erased from your mind. It worries, or encourages, or leads you to question. Sometimes, as happened to me recently, a family sadness makes you reflect on life, and death, and what it is we have to give to those around us.

I am not a lover of funeral homes. Their canned music and overpoliteness, their plush furnishings and remote-controlled doors, and a sort of enforced solemnity, keeping death at arms length, usually make me feel uncomfortable.

But this was different. A simple photograph and a few toys, the warm words of a sympathetic woman minister, and a congregation of different races who had come to share with a bereaved family, turned what could have been a grim grieving into a kind of birthday party. Lots of tears in the room but also lots of laughter—and satisfied hearts going home afterwards.

Austin Michael Banda lived just 141 days. I did not know him but his parents, John, from Malawi, and Sara, from Beaverton, Oregon, are dear friends. He never left the hospital, never learned to speak or write, never was able to live without tubes. He could not eat normally or even sit up. He was in surgery many times. But his life touched dozens of people in a way they will never forget.

His horizons were restricted. He knew nothing of fields or beaches or summer days. But he loved his bath, he loved his stuffed puppy, he loved the music from his tape recorder, and his tastes ran from "Twinkle, Twinkle, Little Star" and the songs of Canadian singer Raffy to Vivaldi's *Four Seasons* and the soothing jazz of Grover Washington, Jr.

At the funeral they remembered, too, the day he discovered his hands, that they belonged to him, that there were two of them, and the pleasure it gave everyone. The large group of mourners was, in part, supporting John and Sara in their loss. But it was more. It was tribute to a unique personality.

His short stay on earth drew out the best from the devoted medical personnel. As his night nurse wrote about her last time with him, "I now see Saturday night as Austin's gift to me, and as my gift to Austin." She referred to the fact that his father liked to call him "prime minister": "You always did have that serious look about you," she wrote. "Yes, you could smile but only when you were good and ready. I always felt fortunate to even get a twinge of the upper lip." Another nurse wrote, "Austin, you touched my life in ways I'll never be able to express. I am so thankful for the time I was able to spend with you. I wasn't ready to say goodbye, I hadn't given up on you. The suffering is over, you're at peace. I love you, little one."

Austin reminded us that there is more to life than achievement and status and possessions. He had nothing but a few toys but he gave richly to all and touched the lives of dozens who were at the funeral and many more who were not.

It was moving to listen to the letter to her son from Sara Banda. I am sure it will speak to many who were not at the service:

> My darling son, Austin, I don't understand why God sent you here for such a short time but I know that one day we'll be together again and then I'll understand and be at peace. You had such a special gift with people. You made so many friends and touched so many lives with your gentle loving spirit. I am so proud to have been your mother.
>
> We had many good times together. I remember a day in early February when you were feeling really well. We were all together in a parent room with your daddy and sister Justine. It was the first time Justine got to hold you. You were so patient with her and the loving looks the two of you exchanged just melted my heart. Justine talks about you all the time. Whenever we pass a brick building she screams from the car seat, "There's Austin's house. Let's go see Austin." I especially enjoyed our bath times together. I loved holding you in my arms and rocking you. You always loved the human touch, whether it was a finger to hold or a face to gaze at.
>
> I'm going to miss seeing you grow up. I would have loved having you track mud through the house and the treasures you could have found outside—snakes, frogs, perhaps catching a butterfly and putting it in a jar. But I know you would have wanted to let the butterfly go free. Just like I must say goodbye to you and set you free. I'll always, always love and hold you dear to my heart. Until we meet again, I know Grandma Gladys and Grandpa Austin are taking good care of you for me.   Love, Mommy.

18 MAY 1989

Facing life

MANY MORE PEOPLE than we imagine are afraid to leave the shelter of their homes. Not because they fear that they will be mugged (although that is a present fear for some) but because they are facially disfigured and don't care to confront the insensitive attitudes they expect to encounter.

Disfigurement is caused principally by road accidents, burns, and surgery. Today sophisticated surgery can often save people who in the past would have died. But until recently the psychological problems created in such patients had been largely overlooked. The reason we do not see many disfigured people around is not that they do not exist in large numbers but because they often shun society because of the strain which is involved.

I hadn't thought about this until we were visited a year or so ago by a remarkable woman, Betsy Wilson, from Concord, Massachusetts. She was so outgoing that we scarcely realized that she had had to have her jawbone replaced because of cancer. As a teacher and a mother of three grown-up children Betsy had written on how hospitals could give better care and support to the young and the aged and now, she told us, she wanted to create a national support group for people like her.

This past week I received in the mail a newsletter from Let's Face It, the organization she has set up as a network for the facially disfigured. Four years ago she had read a book entitled *Let's Face It* by an English woman, Christine Piff, documenting her experience losing her left eye and palate to cancer. Interviewed on television, Christine had launched a support organization, not knowing what the reaction would be. Within four weeks she had received 500 letters. "It was like lifting the lid from a boiling pan and letting out so much anguish, despair, and complete frustration," she said.

Betsy was so struck reading the book that she went to meet

Christine in England. "I realized for the first time that I wanted to talk to others who had dealt with life after facial surgery," she said. Betsy understood Christine's feeling during surgery that she needed someone with whom to share her experience. She understood the need to create more caring families, more sensitive hospital staff, and the right follow-up care from surgeons. She returned home determined to follow Christine's example.

As she made preliminary forays in different parts of the country Betsy was encouraged by the response from people in similar situations: such as a former chief justice from Florida whose entire cancerous jaw was removed, and a woman in Albuquerque who wrote, "I am so excited about your group. I have felt somewhat isolated from the rest of humanity most of my life."

Betsy's newsletter recounts the experiences of others who are facially disfigured and lists resources available to them. Let's Face It hopes to promote public sensitivity to the needs of all people with handicaps. She believes that people can have their appearance altered without its altering their lives, and that being disfigured need not mean being disheartened. Her new friends are learning to improve their looks by using appropriate cosmetics. But above all, she says, they are learning to improve their attitudes.

Perhaps they will be used to help us improve some of ours.

22 APRIL 1988

Black cowboys

When Paul Stewart was growing up in Clinton, Iowa, in the twenties, like many children he loved to play cowboys and Indians. The kids would take turns being one or the other. The only trouble was that Paul was black. When his turn to be cowboy came he was always told he couldn't be, there were no black cowboys. So he was always an Indian. Ironically, the role was right because, as he discovered later, he was part Cherokee and part Blackfoot. But he was not satisfied.

Many years later in Denver, Colorado, he glimpsed a tall black man in cowboy hat and boots. "Who's trying to fool me," he thought. Blacks never featured in the photographs he examined, in the Western novels he devoured, or the Western movies he watched. But this man proved to be the genuine article: he had a ranch outside the city and had ridden on the early trails.

So there began for Stewart a 30-year quest to uncover the truth about the black cowboy. This quest had him following every lead he could to people who knew how it had really been: interviewing, taking photographs, collecting guns, ropes, and the like. He has written two books, *Westward Soul* and *Black Cowboys*, and is the founder of the Black American West Museum in Denver.

Patiently examining census records, which listed facts of race; chasing down rare photographs and documents; conducting interviews with old-timers; he has pieced together a forgotten history. "Paul Stewart mines 'lost gold' with a tape recorder" is how an article in the *Smithsonian* magazine described his work.

Stewart says (and it will be a surprise for those brought up on "white" history), that research and government statistics show that as many as three out of five of all cowboys on the plains may have been black. "The black is very visible in history," he says, "but invisible in the history books."

Historian Stewart was in Portland as guest of the newly-formed Friends of Black Studies at Portland State University. I talked with him after his slide presentation to students. Dressed in a black cowboy hat, he insisted on greeting me with a cowboy handshake, first the little finger, then the thumb, then the whole hand. Aware of some of the controversy over the teaching of history, he told me that he was telling it as it was. He was prepared to back up everything he said.

I had just been reading a book by another historian on this same subject, William Loren Katz' *The Black West*, which has a chapter on the black cowboy. The two men know each other. And many of the same fascinating characters are in that book as were in Stewart's slides.

Stewart told of black pioneers: Barney Ford, an ex-slave who became the fifth richest man in Colorado; Bill Pickett, who invented bulldogging (the wrestling of steers to the ground); Sam Palmer, the first man to ride a buffalo; Clara Brown, who became rich by outfitting gold prospectors against a signed promise that they would share half their winnings; and Charlie Sampson, one of today's biggest rodeo money-winners and a past world champion at bull riding. Katz' characters range from the 5000 black men who helped drive cattle up the Chisholm Trail after the Civil War, to Cherokee Bill, the black equivalent of Billy the Kid, who was hanged at age 20 and whose last words were, "I came here to die, not to make a speech."

Stewart would probably back Katz' contention that there was less prejudice among cowboys than among those in many other lines of work. Cowboys of different races herded together, ate together, bunked together. But black cowboys haven't been treated as well by historians.

Katz spoke to Langston Hughes shortly before he died about blacks in American history. "Don't leave out the cowboys," said the black poet. Katz didn't. And I think through Stewart we're going to hear a lot more about them. There is the prospect of several films soon, he says.

4 DECEMBER 1990

Five Oscars

THE ORIGINAL male chauvinist pig has died.

You might feel this is hardly a worthy way to start a tribute to a friend who has just left us, let alone to a sensitive artist who was honored by his peers, the American Society of Music Arrangers, as the first recipient of the president's award for distinguished service to music, musicians, and the entertainment industry.

But then Johnny Green had a bubbling sense of humor and timing—he once doubled as musical director of the Jack Benny radio show and comic foil specializing in dialects—and would have happily acknowledged this, his own description of himself. It is also a reflection both of his humility and of the remarkable changes in his life, changes which meant that he and his wife, Bonnie, instead of adding to Beverly Hills divorce statistics, stayed together for 46 years.

"He was the best of his kind," remembers Gene Kelly, who frequently worked with him. "There are none like him around any more. He was the granddad of the musical score on every movie." Johnny Green won five Oscars (and was nominated for nine others), as well as a Grammy, a Golden Globe, and an Aggie, the highest award of the Songwriters Guild. For 12 years he was the musical director of MGM, and for 32 seasons conducted the Los Angeles Philharmonic in the Hollywood Bowl, as they played hit songs he had written (the best known perhaps being "Body and Soul"), and his award-winning arrangements for musicals like *Oliver*, *West Side Story*, and *An American in Paris*.

Johnny was a master interpreter of Gershwin who had been his early inspiration. In fact, I recall once his telling us that as a boy of 12 he was taken by his parents to a party for Gershwin, a family friend. Young Johnny was asked to show off his talents, which he did—by sitting down at the piano and playing his own arrangement of Gershwin. Green became a Gershwin protegé, and later attended the premiere of *Rhapsody in Blue* in New York. "The bloody place blew up," he recalled.

At a memorial service for Johnny in Bel Air Presbyterian Church, Los Angeles, in May 1989, composer Sammy Cahn said, "When Johnny was very young, he saw a piece of furniture and asked, 'What's that?' He was told, 'That's a piano.' He said, 'I can play that.' And he did—beautifully. There were some papers on the piano, and he asked, 'What are those?' 'Those are songs,' came the reply. 'I can write those,' said Johnny. And he did. One day he saw a man up in front of the musicians waving a stick. 'Who's that?' he wanted to know. 'He's conducting.' 'I can do that.' And he did. Then there was this building covered with ivy. 'What's that?' Johnny asked. 'That's Harvard College.' 'I can go there.' And he did."

In fact, Johnny went to Harvard when he was 15, majoring in economics, and was always proud of his links with that institution. While still an undergraduate he was doing musical arrangements for the new Guy Lombardo orchestra and also wrote the song "Coquette," which became the biggest sheet-music seller in the country. His father was unimpressed. "You can be a good banker, a good lawyer or doctor and you'll be a proud, respected citizen in the community," he told him. "But there is no bum in the world like an artist who is merely good, and I'm afraid as a musician you are merely good."

Bowing to his father's wishes he took a job on Wall Street, but after 6 months quit to become a rehearsal pianist at a Paramount studio in Long Island for $50 a week. It was the start of his long and honored musical career. In his 70s he was still composing. But he was more than a supreme musician. At the memorial Charles Champlin, *Los Angeles Times* drama critic, spoke of him as a role model and described working with him on scholarships for students. "He was," said Champlin, "a suave urger of people. He could twist your arm and make it feel like a therapeutic massage. One of my most vivid memories of John is this: sheer courage."

Fifteen years ago the composer was commissioned by officials in Colorado to write a symphony to commemorate the American bicentennial and the opening of Denver's new concert hall. Into the symphony, entitled *Mine Eyes Have Seen*, he wanted to put something of his own spiritual journey and of the centuries-long march of faith. And he wanted to show, in the accompanying printed program, parallels and contrasts between secular and Biblical history. He undertook a 6-month crash course in the Bible with the result that he came to know Jesus as the Messiah whom the Jewish prophets had foretold. "So," he said, "this 5000-year-old Jewish intellectual decided to be baptized." That happened on Palm Sunday 1989.

"His Jewishness was terribly important to him," said Dr. Donn D. Moomaw, the pastor of the Bel Air church. "He never for a moment repudiated it. He regarded it as the next step for him as a Jew."

Johnny's wife, Bonnie, thanked everyone who had taken part in the service in a church which had been her home since 1961, his since 1977. I remember Bonnie and Johnny describing at a conference the moving story of how they had persevered in their marriage through tumultuous ups and downs. Bonnie, a statuesque blond, was one of the original MGM "glamazons" and an Olympic-class swimmer. But she also, she admitted, had "a halo as big as the moon." Johnny once called her "a platinum Sherman tank."

After a crisis in which she discovered a blatant act of unfaithfulness she decided not to blow up with the usual ultimatums. "Help me, God, I am making a mess of everything," she prayed. God began to speak to her, she said, and she began to obey. It was so difficult at times that she wanted to die. "The hardest part was forgetting, letting go and moving on—because many of us like to feel sorry for ourselves."

"In my own case," Johnny said, "this required a deep x-ray look at my own spiritual anatomy. When I finally examined the plates I got a rude and shattering shock. I found that all my attitudes towards Bonnie were anchored in self-serving pride, in the conviction of my 'special' intellectual superiority and my 'divine' right to deal with Bonnie from Mount Olympus. I came up head on against the awful truth that I was the original male chauvinist pig. But God gave me the light to see what a blessed thing our marriage could be if I could find the sheer guts to change: to get on my knees and apologize to Bonnie for the stupid arrogance with which I had deprived her of her God-given fundamental rights of full partnership."

Johnny had a trademark—a fresh carnation, which he wore in his lapel every day. He wore it, he said, to remind him of the beauty in the world and of his obligation to protect and extend it if he could. He did that with his life, too. And he will continue to do it with his music.

1 JUNE 1989

3   Run that by me again

This just in: "An Administration spokesman, who asked not to be identified, refused to comment."

Cartoon in National Review

"One thing at least has now been proved beyond all doubt: smoking is one of the biggest causes of statistics."

The Economist

A recent study makes it clear that 50 percent of all people involved in divorce are women.

Have a good one

'TIS A FAMOUS VICTORY. Well, not exactly. It's hardly even a small step for man. Or woman. And yet, for those of us who resent the cold-blooded murder of the English tongue it signifies that not all is lost.

I'm not a Safire or a Kilpatrick or a Newman. In fact, my own English isn't all that hot. I failed my final English exam at school. So I don't get unduly worked up about the misuse of language. And I appreciate the way it is daily enriched by new words and phrases. "Run that by me again" is so much more interesting and up-to-date, if a little ruder, than "I beg your pardon." As Horace wrote almost exactly 2000 years ago, "It has always been lawful, and always will be, to issue words stamped with the mint-mark of the day."

No, it's little things that irritate me. The pilot who announces that we will be taking off "momentarily," which always conjures up for me a picture of a plane that is only going to be a few seconds in the air. "Lasting only a moment" is still the definition for "momentary" in my American dictionary. It's the person who, when I ask how they are, replies, "Good." And I am tempted to respond, "I didn't ask you about your moral character." It's the waiter who says, "Enjoy," leaving me hanging, waiting for the object of the verb.

I guess too many us have imitated the philosophy of that celebrated old English egghead. "When I use a word," Humpty Dumpty said, in a rather scornful tone, "it means just what I choose it to mean—neither more nor less."

Getting the words right is not a religious conviction with me. Though I note that in the Bible it says, "A word fitly spoken is like apples of gold in pictures of silver" and in the Koran it is written, "A good word is like a good tree whose root is firmly fixed, and whose top is in the sky." I quote without comment the school superintendent from Arkansas who said,

"If English was good enough for Jesus, it's good enough for you."

Now, back to the victory. There it was in a news brief in *The Economist* magazine. Apparently a teacher in England became infuriated at a certain misuse of the English language, which, by the way, I hear regularly on TV news broadcasts and read in the columns of our reputable papers in Oregon. It was a sign at an express check-out stand at Marks and Spencer that got his goat. He went into battle and he got it changed. So now the sign, instead of reading "Five items or less," reads "Five items or fewer." I might add for those who have forgotten: "few" denotes quantity, "less" denotes degree. As in, "if there were fewer commentaries there would be less talk." However, I don't think this is a victory we will win here. The fine distinction between "less" and "fewer" is probably too far gone. In which case we will have to cut our losses and concentrate on something else. "Hopefully," possibly?

Hopefully, I haven't worried you. If I have it might be a consolation to recall the words of that great French writer, Voltaire, "Language is a difficult thing to put into words."

23 OCTOBER 1990

A vote for communism

EARLIER THIS YEAR *The Economist*, referring to the United States, ended a lead editorial, "Television seems to have done its best to drive humor out of politics. Can you imagine Lyndon Johnson getting away with half of his witticisms today? If we are all to enjoy the twenty-first century, America must lighten up a bit."

Not a bad bit of advice for election day.

I have a friend in Missouri, George Sherman, who says that as a reporter he listened to thousands of political speeches, many of them by candidates seeking to convince they were the finest examples of political ability since Abraham Lincoln. Only one of those speeches can he now recite with accuracy. He heard it a number of times and on each occasion was even more impressed with it. The memorable orator was H.F. Mundy, a Democrat who served several terms as a county coroner. Each time he was introduced as the next candidate he would rise, smile, and say, "Vote for Mundy on Tuesday, thank you." He never lost an election.

Of course, the smile may have had something to do with it. It certainly did with my mother-in-law, who once cast a vote the family never allowed her to forget. This was in England, with candidates listed just by name, with no party affiliation mentioned. She was met at the polling booth by a smiling young man. When she got into the privacy of the booth, his was the only name she could remember. Afterwards, at home, as my father-in-law went over with her the list of candidates, it was clear that the charming young man she had voted for was the Communist Party candidate.

I have been in many different countries at election time, one of them the island of Cyprus. The country's election law forbids campaigning for 24 hours before polling. It so happened that on this particular eve of election we were being visited by Chief Walking Buffalo of the Stony Indians of western Canada. A priest generously offered to meet him at the airport and show him the villages of Cyprus. This whirlwind tour with the chief in full regalia proved, of course, very popular. At each village large crowds gathered and the chief delivered a message of peace. At one point I asked a policeman to translate for me what the priest was saying in the chief's introduction. He listened. "He's saying, 'Chief Walking Buffalo has come here today to tell you to vote for Archbishop Makarios.'"

Lest any candidates, successful or otherwise, at this election have swallowed too much of the adulation they received from their supporters around the state, I would recall the wise perspective of Winston Churchill. At one big public occasion the moderator of the proceedings leaned over to him and said, "Doesn't it thrill you, Mr. Churchill, to see all those people out there who came just to see you?"

Churchill replied, "It is quite flattering, but whenever I feel this way I always remember that if instead of making a political speech I was being hanged, the crowd would be twice as big."

We are fortunate that at our elections the result is respected by the incumbent who then moves out—in England the same day, in America at the new year. No such luck, if I may allow one serious note to intrude, for the Burmese.

Their plight reminds me of what happened once when Elgin Baylor led the Los Angeles Lakers. He agreed to a vote among the players as to whether to buy blue or gold blazers. The vote was for gold and Baylor promptly ordered blue. Asked for an explanation, he said, "I told 'em I'd give 'em the vote. I didn't say I'd count it."

6 NOVEMBER 1990

Life à la carte

I'VE JUST BEEN to the dentist. "Let me give you some floss," she asked after she had cleaned my teeth, "mint or cinnamon?"

To be frank I had never considered the question before.

I don't know whether it is because I was brought up in the era of wartime shortages or because I am English, but I sometimes find the myriad choices I face in this country exhausting.

In England when I asked for a sandwich I didn't get the immediate comeback, "Rye, wholewheat, sourdough, french, or pita?" One took what one was given.

When I wanted salad I didn't get asked, "Thousand island, blue cheese, ranch, italian, house?" In fact, salads, let alone their dressing, were neglected.

I feel rather like the English character in a cartoon who,

when asked what flavor ice cream he wanted: vanilla, chocolate, or strawberry, responded in a flustered fashion, "Er, you choose." I sometimes do that. Heinz 57 varieties, Howard Johnson's 32 flavors, they've been for long the very essence of the American way of life.

I am not the only one to observe this cultural difference. Jane Walmsley, a New Yorker married to an Englishman, has written what she calls a "transatlantic survival guide" entitled *Brit-think, Ameri-think*. The British, she says, would define the word "anarchy" as "unlimited choice." They would be of the view, "It's part of human nature to be happier when our horizons are limited, someone else is in charge, and we know what's expected of us." That is why monarchs are so useful, she maintains, and the class system survives.

Americans are quite the opposite, she says. Why, they don't even like restaurants with set menus. "The right to substitute a tossed salad for french fries is enshrined in the Constitution. Americans like to live life à la carte."

The just-concluded election would be, for her, proof that for Americans choice is something to be exercised as frequently as possible. That's why, she says, Yanks elect so many people: presidents, governors, judges, senators, representatives, and dogcatchers. And if she is right about Americans' being characterized by lots of choice, then Californians are in the mainstream. This election every Californian, as well as having to choose between the many candidates for office, had to make decisions on twenty-nine ballot measures. If you were from San Diego you had in addition eleven local ballot measures and in San Francisco twenty-five, making a total, one Bay Area resident said, of sixty-one.

British political scientist Ivor Crewe, noting how often Americans go to the polls, says, "The average American is entitled to do far more electing, probably by a factor of three or four, than the citizen of any other democracy."

So there are some advantages to being a resident alien like me. I can't vote and I don't have a bad conscience about it.

By the way, I couldn't decide whether I wanted mint or cinnamon floss. So the dentist gave me both.

11 NOVEMBER 1988

A wreath for Reith

DO YOU KNOW what I am wearing as I deliver this commentary? No, of course you don't. It is one of the advantages that radio has over television. But not so many years ago, even within my lifetime, when the broadcasting of news first started in England, the announcers, as they were called, always wore tuxedos. This was because the imposing and dogmatic first director-general, Lord Reith, a dour Scot, felt it was the proper thing to do.

George Bernard Shaw once wrote, "We don't bother much about dress and manners in England because as a nation we don't dress well and we've no manners." Well, of course he was an Irishman and the Irish don't always get it right about England. How you dress matters a lot in some circles.

When I was a small boy my father would never dream of letting me visit him in the City, the business quarter of London, unless I were wearing a hat. It had a lot to do with doing the "done" thing and with status.

At my London school we were trained early in a dress code. First-year boys wore their school blazers with the middle button done up, second-year boys could undo the buttons or do them all up, third-year boys could put their collars up and, incidentally, put their hands in their pockets, etcetera, etcetera. To this day I still find it hard to talk to anyone with my hands in my pockets.

Our home in London had four floors and an intercom system to connect them. When guests came for dinner I would greet them at the front door, usher them into the coat room, and then pick up the intercom and let my wife know whether to wear long or short. It would not do to embarrass the guests by being too differently dressed from them.

When we came to the United States, and particularly to the Pacific Northwest, we had heard that life here was less formal than in England. When we gave our first dinner party we wondered how to dress. I put on a shirt and tie and a suit and then began to have doubts. So I went into the room that overlooked the driveway, switched off the light, and observed our guests arrive. Sure enough, Cyrus was wearing an open-necked shirt. I rushed back to the room, took off my suit, and made myself thoroughly casual. The doorbell rang. I went to it. And there stood his wife, alone. "Where's Cyrus?" I asked. "Oh," she replied, "he saw through the window you had a tie on and has gone back to get one."

Well, after a few years here I have become slowly attuned to Pacific Northwest ways. I still tend to be a little overdressed on occasions. But I thought I had made real Oregonian progress when I was in the airplane on my way to Washington, D.C. and remembered I had forgotten to pack a tie.

For all you know I may have on beach wear for this commentary. If Lord Reith got to hear of it, I am sure he would turn in his grave.

19 AUGUST 1988

Decadent youth

"HOW DIFFERENT from the present was the youth of earlier days." I wonder how many fathers looking at their children or other people's children make or think of making such a remark. This particular comment comes from the Roman poet Ovid, who lived in the time of Christ, 2000 years ago.

How different and how much alike. It is said that you can give your children all the advantages you never had but you can't stop their growing up like you.

The young people of today have one thing in common with those of my youth and those of ancient Rome, the absolute conviction that they are very modern and their parents fuddy-duddy. I remember as a small boy not being able to understand why my father didn't think a certain cartoon funny. But you should feel the force of my daughter's reaction if I am slow on the uptake when she shows me, say, one of Larson's Far Side whimsies. I guess my only hope with her is that phenomenon observed by Mark Twain: when I was very young, I thought my father stupid. But when I got older it was surprising how much he had learned.

It is true that at times I thought my father pretty antediluvian; his views to be tolerated. After all, what could you expect from someone born in the nineteenth century, well before the invention of radio or airplanes, someone who was a captain in the first World War. He was 40 years old before I was born.

But then my daughter is 40 years younger than I am. To her the second World War, which ended when I was in junior high school, and which with luck she might study about in college, is as far removed from her as the Spanish-American war was from my schooldays.

And the tempo of change is growing perceptibly. In my youth we used kitchen appliances you will now find in the Oregon Historical Society's exhibits. I can recall feeding sugar to the horses, which in London drew the milk delivery carts, watching the lamplighters at work, and seeing cars started with little cranks in front of the engine. In my last year at high school there was just one television set, and a demonstration one at that, in our neighborhood. When I left school I was wearing detachable collars fixed with studs to my shirts.

But if my daughter has children what will they think of her times? Of course, my daughter doesn't consider any more than I did at her age that what seems so modern will one day look so dated. What will my grandchildren say? Perhaps they will say, "They wrote and mailed letters when mum was young and couldn't even see each other when they spoke on what they called telephones. They had to steer cars on roads, they flew in planes, and you should see the old-fashioned clothes they wore and the music they danced to. They even smoked cigarettes." Well, let's not carry it too far.

Let me give you another quotation. "Oh, this age. How tasteless and ill-bred it is." That was another Roman poet, Catullus, almost a hundred years earlier than Ovid.

Such perspectives should help deter parents and children from rushing into judgment of each other. But they don't.

23 SEPTEMBER 1988

Walter Mitty lives

I AM A VERY SPECIAL American. Indeed, I have an impressive letter to prove it. "Dear friend, you are a very special American," it starts. But it's not true. Because even if I were special I'm not American. It is one of those letters that assumes that if your vanity is appealed to you will quickly part with some cash. "I need your help. We are completely funded by voluntary gifts of concerned, civic-minded citizens like you."

I began thinking about this approach in relation to my own country, England. I don't think that sort of appeal would work there. "You are a very special Englishman." First of all, most Englishmen secretly feel that way, anyway. Though they certainly wouldn't admit it. That would be frightfully bad form.

I say, I don't think it would appeal. But I have been away

more than ten years now and am a little out of touch. I remember just a few years ago I saw the former speaker of the House of Representatives, Tip O'Neill, advertising something or other. I can't remember what it was except that he popped up out of a suitcase. I thought at the time "how demeaning," and, "We wouldn't do that sort of thing in England." Then I was in England for a visit shortly afterwards and what caught my eye: the former prime minister, Ted Heath, doing a pitch for cheese.

However, apart from some glaring exceptions like soccer players hugging each other after scoring goals, there is still a certain restraint in England and a reluctance to show emotion. An Englishman told a very sad story at an occasion in our home recently and broke down half way through. We were all terribly moved. He said to me afterwards, "Thank heavens I didn't do that in England. They don't go for that sort of thing."

I read in the current edition of *The Bedside Guardian* an article describing Michael Chang's words of commitment to Christ when he won the French Open (tennis), and quoting the Reverend Drew Wingfield-Digby, the director of the British Christians in Sport movement: "Michael Chang's courage at standing up to be counted was gloried in by all of us. Mind you, in Britain our ministry, culturally, has a more modified way of expressing our devotion and commitment."

In the movie *The Secret Life of Walter Mitty* Danny Kaye becomes for a moment a Royal Air Force fighter pilot. Some of you may have thought it was caricature when he returns from a mission, is asked whether he is wounded and replies, "Just a scratch. I set the bone myself." But it is not so far off the mark.

A while ago the British war cabinet, prime minister and all, were nearly blown to smithereens by an Irish Republican Army mortar attack. The shell landed in the Number 10 Downing Street garden. The chief secretary to the treasury was in the middle of reporting on his trip to the Gulf when there was an explosion that buckled the toughened glass windows just behind the attorney general and the home secretary and let in a blast of cold air. A few yards closer and the never-to-be-forgot Guy Fawkes gunpowder plot would have been eclipsed. What did the prime minister say? "I think we had better start again somewhere else." And so they did, ten minutes later, in another room. What do the minutes of the British cabinet record for that event? "A brief interruption to the war committee of the cabinet took place."

The public approved. So did I. Any greater show of emotion would have been very un-British. And, that letter notwithstanding, I'm a very ordinary Brit.

28 MARCH 1991

Relax, it's just a test

MOST OF YOU will be familiar with the occasional test of the emergency broadcast service: a high pitched noise followed by an announcement. A friend of mine has a variation on that announcement, which I have pinned up on my refrigerator: "This life is a test. It is only a test. Had it been an actual life you would have received further intructions on where to go and what to do."

I wonder how many people feel that way. How much better we would do in life if we came with a set of instructions. Why does each generation have to experiment, perhaps with a new educational nostrum, a new set of moral values, and the next generation has to pick up the pieces?

Are we accumulating wisdom as the world turns or are we always condemned to reinvent the wheel? It is a cliché to quote the words, "Those who do not learn from history are condemned to repeat it." And I notice that those who do so are often fairly selective in what they think they are learning and use the quote to hit over the head someone else who may have learned a different lesson.

But have we not been bequeathed any safe and sure instructions we can rely on?

Certainly not when we follow fashion or accepted wisdom. Why, I have just learned that my carefully considered course of drinking only decaffeinated coffee may be increasing the likelihood of a heart attack. And that warm-up exercises undertaken at the insistence of my daughter do virtually nothing to prevent muscle injuries.

"Racial violence is growing," shouts one headline, "u.s. race relations improving," claims another. The United States is in decline, it's not in decline. There's a liberal bias in the media, according to one survey, it's conservative, according to another. A priest's report saying that love and fidelity are alive and well in America is soon contradicted by a poll purporting to reveal that more and more people are cheating.

Even history is suspect. I mean, now we learn that baseball wasn't invented in Cooperstown in 1846. Recently discovered newspaper reports indicate that by then it was already well established. Joan of Arc's problem, we are told, was epilepsy. Kinsey's findings, according to a new book, are fraudulent. And as for Columbus' discovering America, I won't get into that, at least not today.

All our respected columnists are agreed that something is foul in more states than Denmark. Georgie Anne Geyer says there's no moral authority left in our society. George Will speaks of America's slide into the sewer. David Broder thinks that our trivial pursuits show the aimlessness of society. William Raspberry believes our society is disintegrating into selfish narrow interests.

Where do we turn if these columnists are right? I think that Richard Nenneman, editor-in-chief of the *Christian Science Monitor*, may be right when he suggests that the moral leadership must come not from another Winston Churchill but from Everyman. "If enough of the business, cultural, academic, and political leaders of the world put into daily practice the values they deeply believe in as right," he says, "their collective actions will move the relations of the world's nations a giant step forward."

It is just possible that the simple instruction, which we overlook, and which operates in spite of the polls and papers, is summed up in seven words: as I am so is my nation.

18 DECEMBER 1990

4 Changing attitudes

MY OWN HOME only says the occupant is poor in the world's goods; it does not shout to anyone that I am dark while my neighbor is white. My dog will not tell you that he is dissatisfied with my color, for, real friend that he is, he sees only me. Our canary does not glance around at his audience to ascertain its color before he trills his song. The flowers in my garden do not turn away their bright heads when I walk among them, nor do they withhold a single breath of their sweetness when I pluck them. It is left for people to make a difference.

Kathryn Bogle, in the *Oregonian*
14 February 1937

Our attention span

"FRIENDS, I HAVE an extremely important message that I want to put before you all today."

Those words, spoken deliberately and slowly, took me about ten seconds to deliver. Not much time to convey anything of significance to the listener. Would you believe it, an analysis of the average length of "sound bites," or uninterrupted blocks of speech by candidates, on network evening news programs in the 1988 elections, was 9.8 seconds. Ten years earlier the average length was 42 seconds.

This comes out of research by Kiku Adatto, a fellow at Harvard University's Joan Shorenstein Barone Center, for a book he is writing about TV coverage of the 1968 and 1988 campaigns. The only positive gloss I can put on that is that if we had had TV at the time of the American revolution we would at least have got "Give me liberty or give me death" and, if he didn't speak it too slowly, Nathan Hale's, "I only regret that I have but one life to lose for my country."

We are being more and more programmed to have limited attention spans. I am well aware of it in myself. Television and radio producers won't give more time to people on the air because they say that the public will switch off, or, worse still, switch over to the other channel. But who conditioned them to expect everything to be so abbreviated? Television and radio producers did. And who is going to reeducate us, to wean us away from comic book news. They will have to.

Fortunately, public television and radio are still not taken over by this philosophy, not entirely dependent on ratings, not part of entertainment. But is it possible to recapture the popular media for intelligent thought? Or are those like Bill Moyers just crying in the wilderness.

Lawrence K. Grossman, former president of NBC News,

spoke this year at the dedication of the Edward R. Murrow School of Communications at Washington State University. He said that television news had declined from what Theodore White called a "primordial power" and dominant force to what has been described as a sheep in wolf's clothing, vulnerable to the picture-and-sound-bite machinations of image experts, spin doctors, and media advisors. He suggested that some network news division might replace the softness and happy talk that pervades the airwaves today and try turning to men and women with strongly held ideas and differing convictions about major issues of public policy.

I would like, one day, a network producer to tell the anchor, "What this woman is saying to you is important, let's keep the camera rolling, and we can scrap that footage of that spectacular fire and that feature on that celebrity." Or tell the camera crew, "This politician is staging the event for our benefit, and there's no substance in what he has to say, we'll give it a miss tonight, to heck with the other network, and let's cover that other story we were having to drop." If the networks dared to risk such an approach, we might see a quick shift in the behavior of candidates and we might get to know them better for what they are.

To rectify a situation that has taken years to develop (and the speed of trivialization is picking up rapidly) will not be easy. It will require some very independent-minded people, particularly in management, who will progress, as media authority Fred Friendly puts it, from an attitude of junk news to the creation of an appetite for quality. They would be doing a great service to the nation.

I am glad that public television is studying a plan to offer free and much longer air time to presidential candidates at the next election.

7 AUGUST 1990

American shame

THE ATTORNEY GENERAL of the United States knelt recently at the feet of a wheelchair-bound, 107-year-old Japanese American, Mamoru Eto, and presented him with a check for $20,000 and an apology from the nation. "By finally admitting a wrong," said Dick Thornburgh, "a nation does not destroy its integrity but, rather, reinforces the sincerity of its commitment to the Constitution and hence to its people."

Eto was one of the 120,000 Americans of Japanese ancestry, two thirds of them born in the United States, who at a time of anti-Japanese hysteria after the attack on Pearl Harbor, had been forcibly relocated and interned in what the Japanese American Citizens League has called "concentration camps." Eto was, at the time, minister of the First Nazarene Japanese Church in Pasadena. "They were not death camps," as *Los Angeles Times* writer Betty Cuniberti put it, "but freedom, pride, and dreams died a thousand times in California, in Colorado, in Arizona, and in Wyoming, in the sprawling makeshift camps to which Japanese Americans were herded."

Congress has authorized the payment of $1.25 billion in reparations for what some lawmakers describe as this "American shame." The money will go to about 65,000 people: surviving internees or their descendants. The tax-free money will be paid within the next three years, starting with the oldest of those eligible.

The mass relocation in 1943 followed an Executive Order 9066, signed by President Roosevelt, moving persons of Japanese ancestry away from the West Coast due to "military necessity," so it is appropriate that accompanying each check will be a statement from President Bush: "We can never fully right the wrongs of the past. But we can take a clear stand for justice and recognize that serious injustices were done to Japanese Americans during World War II."

Representative Robert T. Matsui, from Sacramento, spent the first few years of his life in a California camp. About the same time his wife, Doris, was born in a camp in Colorado. Matsui was a sponsor of the Civil Liberties Act, which authorized the apology and the restitution, along with another California representative, Norman Y. Mineta, who was interned as a 10-year-old in Wyoming, and Senators Daniel Inouye and the late Spark Matsunaga. Matsui sees the outcome as a major victory, not only for those who were interned but for the Congress and the country, and an end to an "arduous national march toward redemption." He will not receive any money. He waived that right so that he could vote for the bill on the floor of the House.

Twenty thousand dollars per person represents, of course, but a small fraction of the funds lost by Japanese Americans through relocation or the replacement of lost property or livelihood. But, as another Japanese American said on television, he was grateful for the money but what meant the most was the apology.

What had hurt the Japanese community was the impugning of their loyalty as Americans and the persecution they suffered because of their race. Many Japanese Americans were serving in the u.s. forces while their families were forced to live in camps. Japanese American volunteers fought in the famous 100th Infantry Battalion and the 442nd Regimental Combat Team—which had the highest casualty rates and most decorations of any unit of its size in all u.s. military history.

Speaking at the moving ceremony in the Justice Department, Attorney General Thornburgh said, "I am not unmindful of the historic role this Department of Justice played in the internment. It is somehow entirely fitting that it is here we now celebrate redress."

Representative Matsui and Representative Mineta embraced, in tears, as the audience in the Great Hall sang "God bless America." Mineta said, "Americans of Japanese ancestry

now know in their hearts that the letter and the spirit of our
Constitution holds true for them."

Seven years ago Minoru Yasui, one of those interned, told
some of us in Portland that he was seeking redress because he
believed in America as a land where ultimately justice must
prevail. Sadly, he did not live to see the triumph of what he
fought for. But he was one of those who, as the attorney general pointed out, never lost faith in the system even when it failed
them.

1 NOVEMBER 1990

Frohnmayer's hotseat

I WAS PHONED by a fellow writer last week and asked to demonstrate outside a talk given by John Frohnmayer, chairman of
the National Endowment for the Arts. I wasn't asked what I
thought. It was assumed that I had a certain view. To be frank,
I am astonished how quickly writers and artists who pride
themselves on their independence of thought become a herd of
group thinkers.

Actually, reading some of the placards held up outside the
talk and some of the things said about Frohnmayer by writers,
I'm glad I didn't join the demonstration. It certainly did nothing to further his hope for "a reasonable solution, rather than a
hysterical response."

It seems that anyone who suggests there should be any limitations on artistic freedom (or that there is any higher value
than the right to spill my guts all over the public) is pilloried as
a jackal or a hyena or a kook or even worse, a right-wing
religious fanatic.

The whole issue revolves around the question of federal
funding for the arts and whether there should be restrictions

on art deemed to be obscene. It is not an issue about which I happily comment.

Let me tell you where I stand. I believe freedom of speech is a precious right. It is one of the glories of civilized society. It does not belong only to those with whom we agree or of whom we approve, and it is open, unfortunately, to the most egregious abuse. Which is what some people feel happened with money given to the Robert Mapplethorpe and Andres Serrano exhibits. But I do not believe there should be an unrestricted right to have such abuses funded by the government. That is not censorship. It is common sense. Would you support your money being given to a brilliantly conceived artistic display in favor of Nazism? Or, as Representative Henry Hyde writes in the *National Review*, "Suppose Mr. Serrano's work had involved suspending a Torah scroll in a vat of urine; would any reasonable person have doubted that this was a gross act of anti-Semitism?"

I also happen to believe, I might mention as an aside, that most censorship in this country is exercised not against vice but against virtue. Anyone who wants to push out the frontiers of immorality and pornography will find swifter access to money and publicity than someone who wants to enrich the country's wellsprings of faith and morality.

John Frohnmayer is in the hot seat. It is a no-win situation and one that rightly has to balance the traditional and indispensable freedom of speech mandated by the Constitution and the complicated tugs and pulls of a pluralistic, everything out in the open, modern society. He deserves better than the vituperation with which he was met by some of Oregon's writing community.

I don't know what the future of the National Endowment for the Arts should be. It seems to have done its work well over the years. It has probably funded some poor art but it has also enabled many works of value that needed help to go ahead.

The attacks on it are out of proportion and much political capital is being made of the issue. Somewhere in the whole debate is hidden the question of the purpose of art and the nature of our society in the years ahead. Too big a question to get into today.

I don't think I would ever qualify for one of the NEA's grants. Though if I did I can assure you of one thing: I would not feel demeaned by promising not to make my work obscene.

3 JULY 1990

Today's Pearl Harbor

I ATTENDED an unusual breakfast meeting this week, an open forum of Portland's City Club. The speaker was described in *Fortune* as a low-profile, mild-mannered chairman of a secretive company who has had a Clark Kent-like transformation and is now a "trail-blazing, pulpit-pounding crusader for reform in the public schools." And he surely is. I refer to Brad Butler, former chairman of Procter and Gamble, who was in the city as keynote speaker at a conference titled "Oregon's Children: An Investment in our Future."

"At Pearl Harbor we lost hundreds of our young people," the former navy man said. "But a Pearl Harbor is happening every day. Before you get home," he told us, "there will be four thousand young people who are truly casualties, and there will be another four thousand tomorrow and every day, young people who drop out of school and drop into crime, drug abuse, welfare, draining essential resources from the future of the country. If we don't change the way we develop our human resources, this country," he warned, "cannot be a peaceful democracy in the twenty-first century."

Brad Butler's concerns are not new. All sorts of polls and commissions have delineated the problem. But what may be different is business intervention. There is not time to detail Butler's approach but it could be summed up in the words "accountability, deregulation, and competition." It is not a question of whether the schools can be reformed but whether we will put the will behind it, he said. There are already encouraging examples of reform as business and government get together. The public wants change. But they also want leadership they can trust.

The biggest argument for business people is not that reform is right but that it will pay. "If you haven't got a heart," he says, "you've got a head." It takes more money to keep a young person in prison than in college. If American industry is to compete in the world market place it will have to have a better-trained work force. A dollar invested in education will bring a return of four dollars.

Restructuring our schools has also to be accompanied by early intervention, prenatal as well as preschool. Everything that happens before birth affects everything afterwards. Dropping out begins in first grade. The self-esteem of unprepared children can be so damaged that even though they are present in class they will never "drop in."

Butler's fire is fueled by his own experience in the Baltimore public schools, by the strong obligation to pay back what a generation of teachers had done for him, and by the work of the Committee for Economic Development. He communicates informed and infectious optimism, so much so that by the end of the session one senior Oregonian was nominating him for secretary of education, a suggestion Butler quickly ruled out. He could do more for public education without strings or responsibility, he insisted. From the first day he has never endorsed a profit-making organization or consulted with anyone for money, he has no political ambition, and he does not accept any honoraria.

Rather different from many other public figures one could think of. Everyone went off to work with a little more hope about public education. But, as Butler said at the Oregon children's conference, "If you want it solved in Oregon you've got to do it. Don't wait for somebody else or you'll wait the rest of your life while our country goes down the drain."

9 DECEMBER 1988

Mercy or murder?

IF YOU HAVE an English accent you can get away with murder. Well, not exactly. But certainly an English accent does seem, for some Americans, to convey a sense of authority. Not everyone is fooled.

I was recently greeted outside a downtown hotel with a placard that read "Go back to England, we don't want you here." When I started talking with an English accent some of the language became even stronger. To tell you the truth the placards and the wrath were not directed at me but at a fellow countrymen, and fellow journalist, Derek Humphry.

It is curious to me, and a source of concern to some I have spoken with, that this Englishman should have been accorded a cover on *Northwest Magazine* and was on this particular day the speaker at Portland's prestigious City Club. Humphry is a founder of the Hemlock Society, whose avowed immediate aim is to get Oregon law changed by ballot initiative so that assisting someone to commit suicide would no longer be illegal. He failed to do so in California. Humphry emigrated to the United States in 1978 after helping his wife to die and writing a book about the experience under the title *Jean's Way*.

In his City Club speech Humphry came across to us as a fairminded, resolute individual who has carefully studied his subject and his opponents' arguments. Perhaps the very rationality and apparent sincerity of his approach makes what he puts forward all the more alarming.

Most of us, I imagine, will have had some close relative or

friend who has suffered in their last hours and have wished for them to slip away quickly. Most of us would probably have no difficulty with the withdrawal of some life-saving support when the patient is beyond recovery. But it is a big leap that offends conscience and in many cases religious belief to go from that to sanctioning the killing of a patient. Or, to use the words that are used in arguments on the subject, to go from passive to active euthanasia.

I talked recently with Karl Gunning, a doctor in the Netherlands, the country where euthanasia is perhaps the most socially acceptable. Since 1984 Dutch doctors have not been prosecuted for helping their own patients to die in certain defined circumstances. Gunning is deeply ashamed of what is happening, particularly in a country where during World War II doctors risked imprisonment and deportation for refusing to cooperate in the Nazi euthanasia program. He, by the way, prefers the words "deliberate killing" to euthanasia.

The Dutch Inspector General of Health, he says, estimates that there are 10,000 euthanasia deaths out of 120,000 deaths in the whole country annually. Gunning says that as the number of patients who ask for death is estimated at about 2000 it means that many thousands have their lives ended without their consent. Another Dutch doctor reports that involuntary euthanasia has become so rampant and is so overlooked by the courts that many elderly patients are afraid to be hospitalized or even to consult doctors.

The British Medical Association has concluded that in some circumstances the withdrawal of treatment by doctors is condoned but that they should not be involved in "the deliberate taking of a human life." The cause of euthanasia in Britain received a severe setback 8 years ago when a trial disclosed that Exit, the leading organization lobbying for legalization, had been operating a mercy killing service on the quiet. My impression from reading the Hemlock Society literature is that its answer is to do everything in the open.

Up to now deliberate killing has been regarded by our soci-

ety as abhorrent. If we begin to accept it as a good thing to
solve one kind of problem we will soon find reasons to use it
for others. The pressures on terminal patients will become in-
tolerable and the image of doctors as healers will then be irre-
parably tarnished. To use the Dutch doctor's very Dutch meta-
phor, "If you have a hole in the dike the whole land soon gets
flooded."

4 APRIL 1989

Priests and purity

IN AN ARTICLE titled "The Ethics of Sex," the *Oregonian* invited readers to respond to a set of questions relating to two
hypothetical sexual situations. These were: (one) "You meet a
man or woman that you really like in a bar. Soon you're holding hands, kissing and clutching each other passionately. Now
your partner suggests more intimate activities." And (two)
"You've been dating the same person for several months, but
have not had sexual intercourse. You've both discussed your
sexual histories and feel ready to make a sexual commitment.
There is talk of marriage in the future." The options posed by
the paper were roughly the same for both questions: "You
fulfill your desires, you use a condom, you require an AIDS test,
you abstain."

An overwhelming percentage of the more than 300 people
who replied were for abstaining. Michelle Stein, the paper's
reporter, summing up the majority of opinions, wrote, "Sleep
with a person outside of marriage and you are not only com-
mitting a sin, you are stupid." I was encouraged and am in-
clined to think that there are far more people leading a disciplined life than one realizes from sitcoms and sex therapists,
from song lyrics, romance novels, and talk shows.

After reading the alternatives, I had written to the paper,

"Anyone who has reached the point described in your article has already to a certain extent passed the point of deciding. I was taught by wise and experienced friends that there is a progression to temptation—the look, the thought, the fascination, and the fall. If you wanted to avoid the fall you stopped at the look. Or, to put it another way, if your problem is falling over precipices don't go near the edge." I also added, "Those who accept a commitment to a disciplined way of life have to have moral guidelines and keep wide margins if they are not going to be seduced from their purpose. They might, as a result, never get into the position of having to make the choices you outline."

I mention this because of two things that caught my attention this past week, one a superb and joyful book *Purity Makes the Heart Grow Stronger* by Julia Duin, a local journalist who is now a reporter for the *Houston Chronicle*, and the other a less than superb and rather sad array of clergy who appeared on Geraldo's show (broadcast from Portland) defending promiscuity. I wish Julia had been on their program. She would, I am sure, have made a helpful and challenging contribution.

In her book Julia makes the same point that if you intend to live as a Christian you need to get order into your life and take a look at what you do and don't do. Referring to the pressures that come from TV and books to be less than you know you ought, she writes, "Reading sexually stimulating material while trying to remain celibate is like reading *Gourmet* magazine while sticking to a diet. We only have so much resistance and once our minds are won over to a concept, it is not long before our bodies follow."

Julia's book is directed to the single Christian but can be read with benefit by everybody. She is very honest about her own struggles both with loneliness and with temptation and the victories she has won during the last 15 years. "I still don't think I possess the gift of celibacy," she writes. "But what I did is possible for any single person who can surrender sexual desires to the Lord and find freedom." She believes that a major stand Christians can take that will make people stop and take notice "is our refusal to indulge in the casual sex that our secular generation considers to be a moral right."

Such considerations, such a concept of the battle between good and evil, such a surrendering of sexual desires to the Lord and finding freedom, seemed to be a long way from the minds or possibly even the experience of the clergy on the Geraldo show. They were putting forward a clergy bill of rights that would allow them to indulge in any sexual act whatsoever provided it was voluntary and did not involve violence. Not a word was said about Christ's call for purity. Indeed, in answer to a question they all seemed to see no conflict between the way of Christ and a promiscuous lifestyle.

I was grateful for the common sense of many in the audience who felt that clergy needed to set a standard, that their lives ought to reflect the will of God, that they ought to respect the vows they had taken. And I was grateful after the program was over to be able to reread Julia Duin's book.

25 MAY 1989

Fashion follies

> Be yourself, be yourself,
> How simple life can be.
> If I was supposed to be somebody else,
> Well, why in the heck am I me?

THESE WORDS of a song popular in the 50s come to mind as I observe the spectacle of older people trying desperately to hold back the inexorable progress of age, fighting a last-ditch Dunkirk every inch of the way.

I wonder what the perspective of history will be on our Western narcissism, our excessive preoccupation with what we look like. What an irony, too, that in our lifetime we sent out missionaries to "civilize" those who painted themselves and mutilated their bodies with knives and wore next to nothing. And now we do the same and call it "sophisticated."

What will be the judgment on a society that can produce sixty shades of luscious long-wearing lip gloss, dozens of anti-wrinkle strategies, and offers face lifts, brow lifts, nose corrections, chin augmentations, neck contouring, and tummy tucks, and yet permits millions to go without the very necessities of life?

This being a free society what you do to your own body to make it more pleasing to you and acceptable to others is presumably up to you. If you want to be mutton dressed as lamb or call your natural hair unnatural and fight aging every wrinkle of the way, I guess that's okay. "To dye or not to dye," as Shakespeare might have said, "that is the question." At least for many.

However, we should go into all this with our fashionably colored eyes open. Too many unscrupulous operators are preying on our desire to hold back the hands of the clock with untested and possibly toxic products. Are our lives to be run by what is right or by what is in fashion?

This is surely a good subject for this Older Americans Month, at a time when we are bombarded by powerful advertising trying to make us either ashamed of our bodies or fearful for our health.

One of the interesting papers presented at the recent Portland meeting of the Western Social Science Association was by Monica Morris, English-born professor of sociology at California State University, Los Angeles, who was addressing this very issue.

In 1972 Susan Sontag, in a classic statement about the "double standards of aging," claimed in the *Saturday Review* that contemporary attitudes about age enhanced a man but progressively destroyed a woman. Monica Morris wrote me, "I've been maintaining that the double standard is changing—but not as Sontag might have wished. Now both sexes are equally caught up in the desperate and hopeless desire to remain young forever."

Monica Morris' social science meeting paper was entitled "The case of the incredible shrinking magazine article: social control by emasculation?" She described how a 2000-word article commissioned from her by *Family Circle* was not only cut drastically but considerably diluted in content. One may put this down to space considerations and a change of editor but it would appear difficult, from her experience, to get any convictions published that are strongly critical of what is being pushed by advertisers in family magazines.

In 1987 Monica had read an article in *Family Circle* (which describes itself as the world's largest selling woman's magazine) that gave an alarming description of what happened to your body as it aged. But, to Monica, the remedies put forward were even more alarming. "Here was *Family Circle*," she says, "recommending plastic surgery as casually as a color rinse to deal with the natural changes of aging."

She sat down and wrote an impassioned letter to the editor asking for the opportunity to write a rebuttal questioning what appeared to have become conventional wisdom about age and beauty. "If collagen injections, Minodoxil for thinning hair, body contour surgery, liposuction and the rest are now recommended in *Family Circle*," she wrote, "then our society has lost its values and direction, and image has become more important than substance.

"We should talk," she went on, "about the costs, emotional and financial, of chasing the unrealizeable and focus, instead, on accepting age as normal. To deny, or resent, or feel horror at life's natural processes leads to self loathing. It drains joy from relationships."

Monica received a form letter of rejection—and was so incensed that she wrote to the editor-in-chief suggesting that even as a matter of good public relations her letter deserved a response. The editor-in-chief replied saying that he shared her point of view and asked her to send an article of up to 2000 words.

Monica told Western Social Science Association members that she went to work determined to write a piece that would fit the magazine's style, would make serious points about resisting social stereotypes, and keep to the prescribed length.

She began with horror stories of beauty practices of other times and places like the binding of little girls' feet in China and, closer to home, of women's breasts in the 1920s. She suggested that perhaps in the future, practices we now embrace will be regarded as abuses. "We don't view as 'mutilation' surgery to carve off 'superfluous' flesh or tighten loose skin," she wrote. "We have fluids injected into our breasts to make them larger, or have tissue removed from them to make them smaller. We put foreign objects into our eyes, even if we have 20-20 vision."

She wrote of the use of Minodoxil for thinning hair and also of the huge increase of calcium supplements following advertisements showing women doubling over with osteoporosis as they age despite little evidence that it would slow bone loss. "We give fortunes to makers of sports and exercise equipment, cosmetics, drugs, vitamins, that offer to hold back signs of aging."

She referred to the dangers of cosmetic surgery and noted that cosmetic surgeons were reporting an obsessive dependency on surgery by some patients and that, increasingly, those seeking surgery to look younger were still in their twenties. She made the point that our obsession with thinness may be responsible for the increase in eating disorders. Girls came to believe thin was beautiful as early as age five.

Drawing from sociological literature Monica went on to

urge that we not allow ourselves to be persuaded by others how we must look to be acceptable, loveable, or employable. "We can take control," she wrote. "We can value ourselves, and others, not for thinness, or age, or our blue or green eyes, but for far more important and lasting qualities." It was important to take care of ourselves and stay healthy. This generation would be the longest lived in history. But we had to get our priorities straight.

The editor-in-chief accepted the article saying it was "a winner." Another staff member told Monica, "We never print this kind of statement. It's about time we did."

A publication date was fixed and soon the edited copy came back. All references to plastic surgery and its dangers, all mentions of calcium supplements, and the section on women taking control of themselves, had been cut. "For space reasons," the editor wrote. Then another letter came saying that the article would not be in the issue planned. Space was short and non-timely pieces had to go. It would be used soon, but with more cuts. A new editor was instituting a one-page, mildly controversial essay at the end of each issue. It would run there. The article was then edited a further 25 percent. Gone was any mention of Minodoxil and much other critical material. Even the editor admitted they were "painful cuts."

Four months later the article was published. The final cuts had removed any mention of treatment for baldness for men, colored contact lenses, and the reference to the liberation of women from endless striving for youthfulness. According to Monica "the text now conveyed little that was sociological, and 'blame' for women's condition seemed to be placed squarely on women themselves."

I have read the article as it appeared and it is a good one. And had I not seen what was omitted I would have been satisfied with it. But I would have missed the serious intent and important content that was in the author's mind when she started.

Monica does not suggest that the transformation of her slightly radical article into what she calls "a bland piece of pap" was a conscious plot. She did not even infer in her paper to the Western Social Science Association that the editing was because of pressure from advertisers. But rather that her whole experience revealed the basic sameness of today's media, which have a formula for successful sales, for keeping loyal large readerships of ordinary consumers as targets for the products advertised.

"In doing so," she says, "among the messages conveyed is that plastic surgery is not only an acceptable way to keep looking young, but it is also right and proper that women, secretaries, and housewives, as well as film stars and millionaire's wives, should look young no matter what their age. Aging is to be feared and all signs of aging should be eliminated or reduced by any means available." She maintains that when conflicting ideas are submitted for publication, they must be controlled, diluted, emasculated. In this way, she says, "editors can claim to write articles that 'pack a punch' but readers and advertisers will hardly feel a thing."

In this Older Americans Month Monica Morris tells a cautionary tale worth pondering. As a card-carrying member of the American Association of Retired Persons I applaud her views. Let's be ourselves.

24 MAY & 31 MAY 1990

Where was Agassi?

THERE WAS an absentee at the Wimbledon tennis championships this year—America's star player, 19-year-old Andre Agassi. He was, he said, taking time to refuel. A lot of players, he maintains, get to the point where they feel their tank is empty. Here is a millionaire who admits he is unhappy, a famous young man who covets his privacy, a whirlwind of energy and power waking up the country club, if the Nike ad is to be believed, who longs for peace and quiet. As he faced the prospect of more high visibility, of pressures and criticism, he said he needed to step back and ask the question "Am I ready to handle that yet? Is it really worth it?" He didn't want to plunge in without adequate preparation or he believed he would find himself starting to resent life.

We all need space in our lives. We need perspective. We need quiet. We need time. We need these elements personally and perhaps nationally as well. I heard Daniel Schorr say recently on National Public Radio, "The country stands in great need of repose."

Politicians need these elements. They need them as world events, and particularly the instantaneous coverage of them, speed up, with a voracious media demanding instant comment. They may not have the luxury of skipping their political Wimbledon. They may have to set time aside, as various cabinet ministers I have met told me they do, to draw back, to reflect, before they are inundated at the office by government papers and official phone calls. Or they may have to develop the peaceful heart that can remain serene while, as Kipling might have said, all around are blaming it on them.

Sissela Bok, in her book *A Strategy for Peace* says that it is this interval of hesitation, of reflection, that permits us to think of the moral dimensions of what we do to and for each other; of what we owe to ourselves, our own groups and communities, and to others, even our adversaries. "In the heat of battle," she writes, "there may sometimes be no time for such reflection; at other times issues are so clear-cut that it is not needed; but as conflicts intensify without any end in sight, partisanship transformed by the experience of exceptional violence may numb the capacity for careful judgment, even when it is most needed and when there is time enough to stop to reflect."

Business executives seem to need these elements of peace and quiet most. I have been surprised by the number of companies that are putting time aside during working hours and finding that such uninterrupted times are actually very productive.

We journalists could certainly do with a dose of reflection. I was glad to read a piece on the subject by Maggi White, editor of Portland's *Downtowner*. Talking of the value of taking time for meditation, she writes, "It requires no designer clothes, no special location, no particular time, and can be accomplished by either sitting or walking." I personally prefer to sit with a notebook and pencil so that I don't miss any inspired thoughts that might come.

I have just received through the mail a national magazine with an advertisement for an electronic machine that can help you create what is described as "a zone of calm." It costs $139.95. When a way to achieve quiet is offered at considerable expense you know there must be a real need in the country.

8 AUGUST 1989

No new challenges

"GIVE ME LIBERTY or give me death." That ringing assertion is part of American history. It is a little more memorable than "Read my lips." "No taxation without representation" got a nation up in arms, I am told. "No new taxes" stirs few to action. I could imagine that in the 1880s some vice-presidential candidate may have said, "I knew George Washington. You're no George Washington." Though we have no record of it. In the frontier days, too, they could no doubt have made use of the theme of a "kinder, gentler America."

Perhaps historians in the future will uncover gems of lasting inspiration in our recent election campaign. We may have overlooked something significant in our preoccupation with the nightly one-liners. After all, many contemporaries wrote off the Gettysburg Address as inconsequential. But by and large we all seem agreed that this past election campaign was shallow in content and low in tone. I wonder if the politicians are asking too little of us.

It is extraordinary how selfless and generous American people are when their hearts and minds have been engaged. Recent studies have shown that seven out of ten American households give money to charitable organizations and 48 percent of adult Americans and 52 percent of teenagers volunteer their time to such work, with the most generous givers in relation to income being the poor and struggling. Corporate giving has increased by 257 percent in the past ten years, growing three times faster than pretax profits. And there are 20,000 grant-making foundations. Tragedy anywhere in the world and the Americans are likely to be the first there with relief. Nowhere has this been more in evidence than in the way American hearts and purses opened to the people of Armenia in their agony.

Seventy-five years ago an advertisement in *The Times* of London stated, "Men wanted for hazardous journey. Small wages, bitter cold, long months of complete darkness, constant danger, safe return doubtful. Honor and recognition in case of success." It was placed by explorer Ernest Shackleton, recruiting men for his Imperial Trans-Antarctic Expedition. Five thousand people responded, his niece, Pat Ducé, reports. "It struck a different note from what one sees today," she says, "with all the inducements and rewards held out as a bait to take on a service, a job, an assignment." In a commentary on British television this year, Pat asked, "Are appeals to self-interest overdone? Are they always appropriate for a country which, for all its faults, does have a track record for responding to challenges?"

Her question to Britain might equally apply to this country.

22 DECEMBER 1988

5   Hope in the cities

AT THE BEGINNING of this century 14 percent of the world's population lived in cities. Today a third do so. By the year 2000 almost a half will. And it might seem odd to suggest that what happens in those cities can be affected by what goes on in a tiny Swiss village.

Yet over the past 45 years Mountain House, Caux, 3000 feet above Lake Geneva, has been a meeting place where, in the spirit of Moral Re-Armament, thousands of people have found the perspective and encouragement to come to grips with some of the most pressing problems of our age.

Set up at first as a center for reconciliation after World War II, Caux and its conference facilities now serve thousands of people every year in every area of life, including cities. It was at Caux that I had the chance to talk with most of the people in this chapter.

No endangered species

THERE HAS BEEN a dramatic decrease in teenage violence in the Atlanta area. Lieutenant Collier of the Atlanta Department of Public Safety puts the drop as high as 40 percent and credits the young men of an organization called BTA, Black Teens for Advancement. I attended a conference in Switzerland about urban problems, along with a dozen of these young men and was able to hear their story firsthand.

In early 1989, faced with a marked increase of black-on-black violence in the Atlanta high schools, a dozen young black men decided to organize to send a message of non-violence to their peers. They regarded the situation as a state of emergency. The students began by arranging a meeting with students from a rival high school. Fifty-three attended. Together they adopted a philosophy that violence had no place in any school building, school ground, or community, and that every student should be responsible to discourage violence in his presence. At each successive meeting more attended and by May there were a thousand present from seventeen high schools.

Adults were not permitted to be present so that students could freely express themselves without fear of reprisal. Nor were females, again to encourage freer expression and because the young black men wanted specifically to disprove the label (which they resented) of an "endangered species." News of meetings spread by word of mouth through the same grapevine that spread news of parties, and students would attend social events under the leadership of the founders to spread the word of non-violence.

BTA members subscribe to a creed, which states, "I, being a young black man, do understand that it is my duty to uphold all standards of BTA. I must remain strong and never do wrong, for if I do, it not only hurts me, but my fellow brothers also. I represent my brother and he represents me; therefore, everything that I do and say, represents all brothers of BTA. I am proud, and I am at peace with my brother."

The trip to the conference in Switzerland involved culture shock on both sides, both for young blacks, who had never been outside the country, and for people from more than fifty countries who had never encountered the dress, language, and attitudes of this younger American black generation.

Each of the twelve BTA men arrived with his Walkman. And the first shock for these city kids was the quietness of this Swiss center. It was only a few days before they had discarded their Walkmans and found themselves, to their surprise, listening and enjoying the stories of people from other countries.

I watched a lively lunch where BTA men met with the mayor and the police chief of Poland's second city, Lodz. The mayor said he wanted to take back to Poland some of the things he had learned from the young Atlantans. I watched BTA men cook with a senior Atlanta judge and wash dishes with the police chief from Pasadena. Everyone shared the work at the conference. I saw them crowd round a black man from England who had been in prison, been turned around and was now running a successful cultural and economic center for a difficult part of London.

Several times the BTA had the chance to address the 600 people at the conference. They took the platform decked out in baseball hats and T-shirts (our "battle dress" as one described it). A co-founder of the organization, Feiji McKay, said, "Our aim is to create better individuals who will do God's will, starting with ourselves."

The young men were interviewed at the end of their visit and said their horizons had been enlarged by meeting people of the most varied backgrounds; stereotypes had been dispelled, prejudices removed. As one of them said, "Being stuck in the U.S. you're kind of limited to the kind of people you meet." Another said that they would be returning home concerned not only for their own black people but for suffering people everywhere.

I have just completed a half-hour video about the Swiss conference. It begins with the violence on the Atlanta streets, shows the founding of BTA, and then accompanies the young men as they attend this conference. It is called *Hope in the Cities*.

Earlier this month the BTA men met, on what has been designated by the mayor of Atlanta as BTA day, with some 2000 young blacks. The challenge they now face is to maintain the momentum of the first generation of BTA members as many have left school, some of them going on to college, and to pass on their liberating experience not only to new high school young men but also to the teenage women, and to both sexes at the junior high school level, where the problem of violence is growing.

6 DECEMBER 1990

Who gets shot?

MANY YEARS AGO, when I lived in West Africa, I knew a newspaper proprietor whose motto was: "Independent in all things and neutral in nothing affecting the destiny of Africa." If you substituted Northern Ireland for Africa the motto sums up appropriately the life of a very remarkable Irishman, whom I talked with recently.

He believes that peace will not come to Ireland until the British troops leave, but he is nobody's man, and as he has pursued his independent ways he has encountered the wrath and cruelty of both Protestant and Catholic extremists. He feels, however, he has nothing to defend because he refuses to be part of any power struggle.

Paddy Doherty is from Derry, which is known to Protestants as Londonderry. To Catholics like him the city has been a symbol of discrimination for three centuries. For years a bell used to sound each evening to warn Catholics to get out before the gates closed for the night. They were forced to live in the area below the city walls called Bogside.

During the civil rights campaign in 1968-1969 Paddy took a lead, controlling vast marches. When Bogside decided to barricade itself off with the name Free Derry, he was nicknamed the Prime Minister of Bogside. For he lived at Number 10, albeit Westland not Downing Street. So his nationalistic credentials are impeccable, as are those of his family, which stretches back in time to when there was an old O'Doherty fort that the Protestants destroyed.

As a result of Protestant-Catholic battles and hundreds of bombings in the last 20 years the heart of the old city was torn out. The area was dead. Many Catholics wanted to destroy forever this symbol of Protestant oppression. But as Paddy looked at the unemployed and the apparent hopelessness of their ever finding work (90 percent of the heads of households in Bogside are unemployed) and the apathy, which he characterizes as "frozen violence," he dared to envisage the city not as a noose for his people, as he put it, but as a necklace to adorn the area. The latent talents of his young people and his own training as a carpenter could be used to rebuild. The result has been extraordinary.

Two years ago the Royal Institute of British Architects and *The Times* of London ran a competition for the best inner city renewal in the United Kingdom. There were 180 entries. Derry was the easy winner, its achievement described in a *Times* headline as "a new heart for the divided city." For Paddy has been able to enlist skilled craftspeople, each training unemployed youngsters, to renovate the historic buildings of the city. He began by setting up an old workshop in a building that had been unoccupied for 14 years. He soon discovered how talented the young people were. In the first period 300 tons of rubble were cleared. To date Paddy and his fellow workers have rebuilt sixteen buildings, establishing shops, living quarters, and craft centers. Some of the first trainees are now running their own small businesses. A center for the performing arts is under construction and twenty-five more projects are on the drawing board.

One of the first buildings restored, which dated from the seventeenth century, houses a center which focuses on the needs of the third world. Upstairs there is rented accommodation to encourage people to live in the old city center again. Paddy feels that exposure to other cultures broadens the horizons and hopes of his young people. When he had an opportunity to take some of the youth overseas he chose India not the United States. He didn't want to show them wealth and have them return dissatisfied but he wanted them to realize that though Ireland is the second poorest country in Europe it is the sixteenth richest in the world. (It is interesting to note that during the 1985 Ethiopian appeal the Irish donated the most per person of any country and within Ireland Derry gave the most.)

Paddy, whose official title is project director of the Northwest Centre for Learning and Development, has the backing of the city council and the department of economic development. Funds are administered by a trust whose trustees include Catholic and Anglican bishops.

"What I have tried to do," says Paddy, "is to match the unemployed to the needs of the area, and use government funds to make up the difference." He has been able, for instance, to secure generous grants covering 50 percent of expenses from the European Community's Social Fund. And three historic buildings have been restored with financial help from the United States and named in honor of the donors: Boston, Minnesota, and Philadelphia. This u.s. participation could, he suggests with a smile, be expanded.

Although Paddy has been seared by the past and, as he admits, is slow to trust, he has not been soured by it and is optimistic about turning around the fortunes of his people. He has a personal stake in thirteen children and thirty-one grandchildren. His credo: "We should not have millions of people unemployed when there's so much work to be done." He says, "It requires imagination and courage, and politicians to have faith that people can do things."

Paddy has these attributes—and a sense of humor. To receive the civic award from Prince Charles he had to go, at some personal risk, to London. At the ceremony Prince Charles told him, "I would love to go to Derry but they might shoot me." "That they might," he replied. "You'd better let me go first and see if they shoot me for meeting you." He told *The Times* that as a Republican he had no problem receiving the award from the Prince: "My line, the O'Dohertys, is as long as his line."

I suspect that Paddy takes particular pleasure from the fact that one of the buildings that has been completely restored, and is so admired by American tourists, is the O'Doherty fort.

13 OCTOBER 1988

Triumph over circumstances

TEN YEARS AGO Leonard Johnson, a black Londoner of West Indian background, was a guest of Her Majesty's government. Or, to put it less euphemistically, he was in prison for theft. Last month Her Majesty's son was his guest as Prince Charles came to open the £5 million Bridge Park Centre of which Leonard is chairman.

Bridge Park Centre is in the heart of the London borough of Brent, which has the largest black population in Europe. It contains a sports arena seating 1500 people, units for thirty-two small businesses, a gymnasium and squash courts, a restaurant and bar, a theater and recording studio, and a nursery, and is used by more than 6000 people a week.

But in 1981, before Johnson and his friends went to work, it was just an abandoned London Transport bus depot. The only center for black youth was the council-run "Annexe," as it was called, whose budget allowed for buying a new table tennis table every few years.

I met Johnson as I was preparing to chair a session at a conference on the problems of cities. I remember him in part because he was objecting, understandably from his point of view, that senior police officers were being given more time to speak than were he and his colleague, Lawrence Fearon, and I was trying to sort out a fair balance.

Johnson and Fearon had met shortly after they came out of prison. They discovered that they both had undergone a remarkable change behind bars. Johnson, serving a 4-year sentence, had had what he called a "Pauline conversion." After mocking religion, God had come into his life. Fearon said that something mysterious had happened to him that he wanted to explore further. They began to consider what they could do for their community. They formed the Harlesden People's Community Centre and called a meeting to solicit ideas on what was needed. The ideas they got that night have now been realized in the Bridge Park Centre.

They began by revitalizing the Annexe and enlisting the help of another club, which was mainly white. They also established a basis of trust with the police and, indeed, prevented wholesale destruction in their area at the time of the Brixton riots. They took their message to drug addicts and illegal drinking shops. They had their meetings broken up by drug dealers. They even had to contend with a dishonest financial officer who embezzled some of the money they had raised. But their faith in God's plan kept them going. Whereas Johnson used to say that he and his fellow blacks were "rats in a ghetto, kept there by whites," his new message became, "There's no point blaming others for the state we are in. We have to stand up and work it out for ourselves."

As their work grew, larger facilities were needed, and with the backing of the local authorities, whose confidence had been won by their leadership and integrity, they looked around for a building of their own. This is when they found the empty bus garage.

Had this center been the initiative of outside agencies it is doubtful if the young people of the area would have been interested. It was their own creation. And it was their enthusiasm and strength of character that enlisted outside money, including a large chunk from the European Community's Social Fund. One of Brent's senior officials said, "It wasn't so much the project we thought worth supporting as the group of people who put it forward."

An article in *The Times* of London, describing the development of the center and the spirit of enterprise of Johnson and others, concludes, "Bridge Park's real significance may be as a message of hope to other black communities." Reporter Andro Linklater believes that there is no precedent in Britain for someone such as Leonard Johnson. "It has always been to the United States one has turned," he writes, "for that extreme example of triumph over social circumstance."

Perhaps the United States could do with more such triumphs today, too.

27 JANUARY 1989

Listeners to a city

FROM TIME to time in Portland we have been visited by a remarkable older couple from that other city of roses, Pasadena. These visits by John and Denise Wood have always drawn particularly appreciative comments from those who take responsibility in community affairs.

It is perhaps appropriate in this Older Americans Month to say a word about their approach, which is described in a new book entitled *Making Cities Work—How two people mobilized a community to meet its needs*. It is written by Basil Entwistle and published by the Hope Publishing House.

During 17 years in Pasadena this older couple has quietly and persistently gone about bringing fellow citizens together to tackle the other side of the city, the problems that are not featured in the Rose Parade: the drugs and gangs, the high unemployment among minority youth, and the children raised in poverty without proper health care. *Making Cities Work*, according to Pasadena Mayor Bill Thomson, "is a blueprint for the citizen action that America's cities need."

The Woods' legacy is seen in the Community Skills Center, which trains 4000 people a year; the Commission on Children and Youth, which has become a major advocate for the welfare of the children; and Day One, which is addressing the problem of substance abuse. Denise set up, through her Episcopal church, the Office for Creative Connections, the name of which in many ways embodies their message.

I have a feeling that much of the success of their work can be attributed to their character, and to attitudes developed during a long life of service to others. But the Woods themselves maintain that anyone can do what they have done.

In a foreword to *Making Cities Work*, Donald Miller, associate professor of social ethics at the University of Southern California, identifies four essential ingredients in their approach: they are wonderful listeners, they refuse to be confrontational, they are honest in their assessment of people and issues, and they have a bountiful expectancy that refuses to accept despair or hopelessness.

The most interesting part of the book is what the Woods describe as "the mindset," which they recommend in anyone who wants to come to grips with the needs of a city. Let me pass on their ten points:

1. Hold to the expectancy and the determination that you and others can make a difference in your community.

2. Study the city by listening to its people one-by-one to gain a living picture of the city's needs, strengths, and possibilities.

3. Reveal the city to itself—the pain, the facts, the hopes, and the moral imperatives you have learned—not in name-calling and blaming, but neither in watering down the truth.

4. Think and speak for the whole city.

5. Bring people together, not in confrontation but in trust, to tackle the city's most urgent needs.

6. Build on the agencies and the people who are already at grips with a given issue and, where need be, encourage new initiatives and coalitions.

7. Take care of the care givers of your community so they know they are not alone and can receive the citizens' support they need.

8. Aim to build lasting relationships.

9. Know there is more power in appealing to the very best in people rather than the worst.

10. Persist when everything seems to fall apart, be conscious that it takes patience, perseverance, and passion to move a city.

15 MAY 1990

Taxi challenge

MY WIFE, Erica, recently read a story on Public Radio's Golden Hours entitled, "Chico the Street Boy." It is the adventures of a youngster growing up in the *favelas*, the shanty towns around Rio de Janeiro. I did not expect so soon afterwards to meet a young man who mirrored Chico's story, and to meet him at a conference in Switzerland on the theme "Getting to the root of the crises in our communities."

This real life Chico is called Reginaldo. He is 32, and married with four children. He is a taxi driver and member of the board of an association of eighty families. To listen to this calm, self-assured, open-faced youth you would have very little idea of the circumstances of his upbringing and what he had to overcome to be, as he calls it, "reintegrated into Brazilian society."

Reginaldo was born in a poor family, his father a truck driver, his mother a domestic servant. His parents worked 12 hours a day to get food for the five children. When he was 10 his mother died and his father, unable to take care of him, sent him off to an institution more than 100 kilometers away. After a year Reginaldo escaped, hidden in blankets, and walked most of the way home, only to discover that the home had been sold and his father gone.

That was when his vagrant life began, moving from house to house, railroad car to railroad car, street to street. He sold ice cream and lemons to survive, began to take drugs, and by the age of 14 was a pusher of cocaine in the shanty towns. Robbery was a way of life for him, and he suffered at the hands of others, sometimes assaults by criminals, sometimes by the police. "I was deep down in a vicious life," he told me. "I was totally marginalized." On one occasion, under the influence of drugs, he got into a fight. A man drew a gun on him. Weaving to avoid the bullets he went at him. Blood was pouring from a chest wound as he grabbed the gun from his assailant's hand and tried to shoot him with it. The gun wouldn't go off. A month and a half later Reginaldo caught up with the man again and shot him four times. The man spent 4 months in the hospital. Twice Reginaldo was sentenced to prison.

In the midst of this kind of life Reginaldo was taken on by a local family who wanted to help him. For 4 years they persevered. "I thank God for putting this family in my way," he says. "Despite all the problems I caused, they did not give up. They did not write me off. They prevented me from doing silly things. And I was freed from drugs."

Determined to start a new life, Reginaldo began to help those around him. His own partially built house was one that was razed by the authorities trying to stamp out squatters. He began to work with an association of shanty-town dwellers. It took time before they would really trust him. Knowing his past involvement in crime, they suspected that he was coming into their community to push drugs. But at 24, he was elected to their board. He was in a position to help get results for the shanty town: water and electricity, a social center, telephone, road resurfacing, and proper brick housing. "I wanted to make up for all the wrong things I had been doing," he says.

In his concern that other children did not go through what he did, he has helped create a sports club to get them away from drug pushers, and a junior housing association where they learn that money has to be earned. He is their tutor, and he organizes activities to raise funds. The children assist the members of the board in their work.

Twelve hours a day Reginaldo is at the wheel of his yellow-and blue-striped taxi, a 1986 chevrolet that he owns. He is a member of an association of 250 cabs.

Recently, during a bus strike, many cab drivers overcharged stranded passengers. But Reginaldo wanted his new attitudes to be reflected here too. He refused to capitalize on the misery of others. As I heard him tell this international conference, "If I overcharge, say a doctor, he may then overcharge his patient, say a storekeeper, who will in turn raise prices in the store. And I," says Reginaldo, "may be the customer."

Invariably Reginaldo's passengers will get into a conversation with him and learn about his past life. Sometimes it causes them to rethink their attitudes. In the early hours of the morning, for instance, Reginaldo may be found looking for fares in the wealthier part of Rio near Copacabana beach. On occasion a passenger has pointed to youngsters sleeping on the streets and said something like, "Look at those good-for-nothing people. They just don't want to do anything." And Reginaldo has turned and said, "I was like that." And if they are interested he then tells them his story. "Many people," he says simply, "become aware they had wrong concepts."

4 OCTOBER 1990

Sewing machine diplomacy

I RECENTLY RECEIVED a clipping from Zimbabwe's *Harare Herald*. There was a five-column article about an old friend of mine from London, Irene Owens. In the accompanying photograph she was sitting with Amai Mugabe, the wife of the prime minister. Both had their hands on a sewing machine.

Some senior citizens seem to be satisfied with aerobics, or adult education, or developing new skills. But not Irene. Moving into retirement, she wanted her life to count, wanted to do something for others. For many years she had been taking time each morning in quiet to see if God had something he wanted her to do. Obedience to the thoughts she got has led to unexpected adventures.

Twenty years ago Irene's mother (whom she had looked after for 10 years), died and so Irene had to move. She found a new apartment in a multi-racial suburb of London. "Before I moved in I saw many black faces looking at me from the house next door," she recalls. "I had never lived next door to another race. I thought I was a good Christian and had no feelings of discrimination." She was muttering, "Oh, dear, oh, dear," as she returned to the home of a friend with whom she was staying. "What is the trouble," her friend asked. "I thought I had no feelings about living next door to colored people," she explained. "Well, you have," said her friend. The next morning in her time of quiet Irene had the thought, "Supposing the one thing you don't like about your apartment is the reason God wants you there. Britain is a multi-racial society and you need to hold out the hand of friendship to other races."

It was in that spirit she began community building. She led a busy life, was involved with the Westminster Theater in London, which is dedicated to reinforcing the moral character of the country, and, after retiring, even visited Australia. On her return, however, she found life rather dull. "Classes in cake decorating, dressmaking, how to keep fit in retirement," she says, "didn't quite fit the bill." Again in a quiet time she thought, "Pray for a new purpose and plan." She happened to mention this in a letter to a friend in Zimbabwe. Irene soon received an invitation to come and help in that newly independent country. "Well," says Irene matter-of-factly, "it's no good asking God for something and when he sends it saying, 'No thank you.'" So she went for 8 months.

When she returned to England it was a time of strained relations between Britain and Zimbabwe, with Britain threatening to cut off aid. She decided to write to Robert Mugabe, the Zimbabwean prime minister, expressing her distress about the situation. "Remember many Britons love Zimbabwe," she wrote. To her surprise she got a warm letter back. On a further visit to Zimbabwe she plucked up courage and asked for an appointment with Mrs. Mugabe. Representing nobody, she wondered what she should say. But she had the thought, "Ask her what the women of Britain could do to help her women?" Mrs. Mugabe's face lit up. "Look at all these letters on my desk," she said. "We're trying to form cooperatives and clubs to teach our women skills." She explained that many had failed to get formal education because they had participated in the independence struggle. Could Irene, she asked, raise money to buy a sewing machine in Zimbabwe.

Back home Irene organized a sale of cakes, marmalade, and nearly new clothes and raised £100. Mrs. Mugabe, in a letter of thanks, said the money would go towards a sewing machine for twenty-seven women who had been prostitutes and who were going to form a cooperative, raising chickens and making school uniforms.

One day Irene saw, in a local shop, a new machine for sale for much less than it would cost in Zimbabwe. She didn't see how she could raise the money to ship it but if she bought it, she wondered, could Mrs. Mugabe find a way of collecting it. "I will be in London next week, thank you for the machine," replied Mrs. Mugabe promptly. That week Irene mentioned at her church Bible group what had happened. Two women immediately offered second-hand machines, another group in the same suburb offered one, and another person added, "My mother is ninety. She bought her machine sixty-six years ago when she married. She would love it to go to Africa." By the time Mrs. Mugabe arrived in London there were five machines ready for her to take back.

I have just heard from Irene who says they have now sent 190 machines—and they often get wonderful letters from the women who are using them. One group said, "We danced all day when the sewing machine arrived." She reports that with the help of money from Sweden the first group of women now have houses built for them by Mrs. Mugabe so that they can live with their children off the streets. They are getting 90 to 100 Zimbabwe dollars monthly from their cooperative and say they will never go back to their old life. "Recently," Irene adds with satisfaction, "they have sent money and clothes to the women in Mozambique."

So when Mrs. Mugabe comes calling in the embassy limousine to Irene Owen's South London apartment neighbors are no longer so surprised. The *Harare Herald* writes of her, "She is a deeply religious woman with a strong sense of service and of the need to bridge the racial divide. The usual retirement pursuits, however worthy, left her unfulfilled. The project which she runs, without any financial or institutional support, has given point and direction to her life and the satisfaction of knowing that her initiative, combined with Amai Mugabe's enthusiastic support, has helped provide a new and more fruitful life for many Zimbabwean women."

3 AUGUST 1989

Why hall of famer came home

I RECENTLY MET Willie Lanier, a former line backer with the Kansas City Royals and a member of the Football Hall of Fame. He is a successful stockbroker with a leading investment house in Richmond, Virginia. That in itself is not particularly surprising except that the black sportsman had left Richmond as a young man vowing that he would never come back unless his family wanted to view his body prior to interment.

It is a measure of the changes that have happened in this southern city, which whites remember as the capital of the Confederacy during the Civil War and blacks as the capital of slavery. It is where I lived for nearly a year before coming to Portland, and I was back for a visit.

Eleven years ago, when I was in Richmond, it was clear that changes were coming rapidly. For the first time the city had a black mayor, Henry Marsh, who in his acceptance speech said that Richmond could be "a model for the nation in determining how a city government can operate free of discrimination on the basis of race, religion or sex." Arthur Ashe, the city's best known son, who made headlines across the country when he was not allowed to play tennis on the Country Club of Virginia courts, and, like Lanier, left the city, told me in 1979, "Things are a lot better than they were and there's every indication they're going to be better tomorrow."

Ashe's prediction has certainly come true and Marsh's vision is beginning to be fulfilled. Not that enormous problems do not remain: for instance the wide disparity of wealth. A recent study showed that, of forty-three American cities with populations between 150,000 and 450,000, Richmond's West End was by far the richest neighborhood of its size while the poverty of the poorest part of Richmond was exceeded only by parts of Atlanta.

I heard Robert Corcoran, who has worked for a number of years with the Richmond Urban Institute, tell a Canadian conference on community building about the new mood in his city. It had come about, he said, partly through changes in the law and changing demographics, but largely through the influence of a committed group of people of all backgrounds, mostly outside the political and economic power structure, who were "prepared to be honest about the past and present wrongs, ready to face the necessary change personally, ready to forgive and ask forgiveness."

Corcoran said that when he moved in it seemed important to him and his wife, Susan, both whites, that they choose to live in a part of the city where their home could be a place of renewal for the community. Twenty years ago in their neighborhood there had hardly been a black family. When the first ones moved in real estate agents had tried to encourage whites to sell out. Indeed, one white former city councilor did leave under cover of night. "But thanks to some courageous leadership," he says, "it is now the best-integrated section of the city." They use their home to bring people together.

Corcoran told the conference that he felt there were four essential ingredients for effective community building: a positive vision of what a city can be; a willingness to take risks and build a bridge with those of differing backgrounds; a belief that even the most difficult people really can change; and a decision to take enough time to seek the creative insights that God can give into relationships with people and the needs of the community.

14 AUGUST 1990

Happy birthday, Dublin

FOURTH OF JULY celebrations are pretty routine compared with the birthday party the Irish are having to mark the 1000-year anniversary of the city of Dublin. It will be the high point in a year of $9 million worth of celebrations, encompassing 1200 events, which by year's end will probably draw a quarter of a million extra tourists to this historic city.

My mother was from Dublin, and emotionally I sometimes feel closer to my roots there than in England. In fact, I have far more Irish mementos to hand: the key to Dean Swift's watch (although I can't imagine how anybody would prove its authenticity); letters from the great champion of Catholic emancipation, Daniel O'Connell; a 1903 poster carrying King Edward VII's message "to my Irish people"; and sketches by Grace Gifford, who married Joseph Plunkett the night before he was executed in 1916. As I write I sit surrounded by sketches by Irish portrait painter Sir William Orpen, which decorate letters to my grandfather, who was registrar of Dublin's Metropolitan School of Art.

My mother was named Erina after her Dublin neighbor, who was the wife of Tim Healy, who in 1922 became Ireland's first governor general. Erina is our daughter's middle name. It was a happy experience to stroll with my mother through Phoenix Park, Europe's largest urban park (where more recently a cross has been erected to mark the visit of the Pope), and to wander around picturesque squares and admire the colorful Georgian doorways, to saunter by city landmarks like the Abbey Theatre or the General Post Office, and past the shops on Grafton Street, which has been, to use a horrible word, pedestrianized or freed of traffic, as part of the city's spruce up for the millennium.

As my mother walked she would point out places associated with her childhood, particularly her days growing up when the country was fighting for independence. She showed us where her school was occupied by troops battling it out with the rebels, and where machine-gun fights took place over the roof of her home. On one visit to Dublin my wife and I stayed in a hotel that had been my grandmother's home, where the family had lived for 400 years; on another we stayed in the historic Provost's House of Trinity College, for the then provost's wife had been my mother's best friend.

In the earlier years of this century, when my mother was at school, our family was all that was unpopular: Anglo-Irish, Protestant, land owners, with a tradition of service in the Royal Irish Constabulary. My grandfather was told to leave the country at independence or be shot. Another grandmother's home had gasoline poured through it and was then set on fire. All that remains are its stone walls.

My mother was, for a time, bitter about the treatment of her family, but she came to realize that it stemmed from the self-centered way many families like ours had lived in the country. She felt that this was something she would like to put right. In later years she became a force for unity between Catholic and Protestant. Indeed, eventually my mother, who had been brought up in the Church of Ireland, joined the Catholic Church.

I'm sorry she is no longer living and able to enjoy the festivities: the cutting of the 1000-candle, record-sized birthday cake, the street parties, the Lord Mayor's parade and other festivities. As I say, "Happy birthday, Dublin," I am grateful for that heritage and also for the fact that it was her youthful, first-hand experiences of war in Dublin that led directly to my being sent as a small boy to the United States for safety during World War II. I had a happy first introduction to this country.

8 JULY 1988

6 Portraits of hope

THERE EXIST some evils so terrible and some misfortunes so
horrible that we dare not think of them, whilst their very
aspect makes us shudder; but if they happen to fall on us, we
find ourselves stronger than we imagined; we grapple with
our ill luck, and behave better than we expected we should.

La Bruyère, 1688

Our way has always been to try to make friends of the enemy
when the guns fall silent.

Laurens van der Post

Wisdom behind bars

I HAVE NOT yet had the chance to meet Irina Ratushinskaya, a leading writer of her generation in the Soviet Union, but I am fortunate to have an autographed copy of her book *Grey Is the Color of Hope*. For some reason this gripping account of her life in a Soviet labor camp has not yet caught on here. (She was imprisoned because of her poetry when she was only 28 years old, and nearly died from maltreatment and the hunger strikes she endured to call attention to the abuse of human rights.) In Europe her book is a best seller, with more than 70,000 copies sold in Sweden alone. The London *Sunday Times* made the book its paperback of the year. Its reviewer wrote, "Serene as well as defiant, Ratushinskaya's memoir is a classic of its kind. She illustrates the fundamental human appetite for song, for the freedom of spirit it asserts and its power to make light of brute authority. What distinguishes her book is its clear-sighted perception that the apathy induced by oppression is what kills the roots of the soul and guarantees evil its success."

From reading the book's most excellent English translation you really get a sense of this indomitable woman and her irrepressible spirit. Irina had received the longest sentence for political crime of any woman since the days of Stalin—7 years of hard labor to be followed by 5 years of internal exile. After 4 years she was released under pressure from the West just before the Reykjavik Summit in 1986. She refuses to hate. Reviewing the book in *Christianity Today*, Ellen Santilli Vaughn writes, "Her story is much more about freedom than confinement: a freedom born of hope, trust in the will of God, and refusal to yield to the will of oppressors. And that, in the end, is why Irina Ratushinskaya could offer her KGB escort a cup of Russian coffee the day she came home from prison."

A friend of mine has recently taken her on a tour of British schools, where the enthusiastic response to her convictions surprised everyone. She would speak for 8 to 10 minutes and then field a flood of questions. One boy asked her why she hadn't signed the piece of paper asking for "pardon" and then resumed her activities once free. "Because," she said, "the first little compromise may seem a little one but once you start it changes you. It always leads on to bigger ones."

In her book she pays generous tribute to Alexander Solzhenitsyn. "Thank you for your priceless counsels," she says to him. "Who can say whether Igor and I would have had the presence of mind to burn all letters and addresses while the KGB hammered on our doors, had we not read your works? Or would I have been able to summon sufficient control not to bat an eyelid when they stripped me naked in prison? Without you, would I have grasped that cardinal principle for all prisoners of conscience: 'Never believe them, never fear them, never ask them for anything?'"

Since her arrival in the West, Irina says, people frequently express surprise at her ability to recite her poetry from memory and at the ease with which she answers questions. She points out that this is because her first large audiences were other prisoners crammed into carriages where not everyone could see her, only hear her voice. Poetry had to be spoken in as straightforward a manner as possible and the questions answered simply, without trying to be clever, the same way she now does in English. She describes how at every transit stop she tried to resurrect the full index of her poems. With everything confiscated only memory could protect her poetry.

Irina is a humble person. At one point she writes, "Thank you, Lord, that it fell to my lot to endure the rigors of prison transports, to hide poetry and books from the KGB, to languish in punishment cells and starve. Only when I entered into open combat did I realize how much help I received from almost everyone I encountered. So many different hands, young and old, slipped us bread when we were exhausted by hunger, so many different eyes smiled at us—grey, brown, blue. And in the wondrous realization that they were on our side, and not on the side of our tormentors, I shed my youthful pride, and the arrogance which might have destroyed my soul melted away." One of her poems reads, "I thank you, rusty prison grating, And you, sharp, glinting bayonet blades. For you have given me more wisdom than learning over long decades."

Irina and her husband Igor, an artist and engineer, now live in London. They travel a lot and are engaged in the work for human rights. She would prefer to be writing. But she says that only when the last political prisoner is released in her country will they be happy to shut up and rest a bit. "But we have no right to do so before that," she says. She has a new book coming out in the spring of 1990 entitled *In the Beginning*. It is about finding faith in an atheistic society. "My teachers told us over and over again there was no God," she says. "Because they felt they had to keep telling us, I knew he must exist."

Edward Ericson, author of *Solzhenitsyn—the Moral Vision*, writes, "My reaction to this couple was much the same as my reaction to Solzhenitsyn and his family when I met them. Here are cultured East Europeans who have become the more refined for the crudities visited upon them. Here are persons of capacious soul and sharp insight, of unshakable dignity and enormous integrity. There simply cannot be many who are their moral betters."

1 MARCH 1990

Instant Swedes

IN JEWISH FOLKLORE there is a tale of thirty-six righteous men, who are the minimum number of righteous men in each generation, because the world exists on their merit. Such men appear to the Jewish community at times of great danger, using their powers to defeat its enemies.

Many see the work of Swedish diplomat Raoul Wallenberg, in saving the lives of 100,000 Hungarian Jews from Nazi death camps in 1944, in that folkloric context. Indeed, he was called by one author, John Bierman, the "righteous gentile." Nobel Laureate Elie Wiesel, in the preface to the book, *With Raoul Wallenberg in Budapest*, wrote, "I do not know what place Raoul Wallenberg occupies in the history of his people; but I do know the place he occupies in ours: it is a place reserved for a man embodying our thirst for justice and dignity and, above all, our quest for humanity."

Swedes are, in fact, justifiably proud of Wallenberg's role. They see his place in the context of Sweden's honorable world humanitarian role, which in turn is an obligation imposed on them by their 174 years of peace. This was a point emphasized by Per Anger, the author of *With Raoul Wallenberg in Budapest*, when he spoke in Portland at an event to honor the Swedish lifesaver.

In Budapest Per Anger was second secretary in the Swedish Legation as World War II was nearing an end. He and a staff of five faced the problem of saving the lives of 750,000 Jews who were threatened with extinction by harsh Nazi policies. "There was nothing written in our diplomatic book of instruction which told us how you can take under your protection citizens of another country," he says. They managed to save a few hundred people and sent urgent messages to Sweden for help.

Fortunately their plea coincided with the search by the u.s. Embassy, world Jewish leaders, and the Swedish foreign office to find someone who could direct the operations of the War Refugee Board, whose priority was the safety of the Hungarian Jews. Raoul Wallenberg was chosen.

On 9 July 1944, 32-year-old Wallenberg arrived at the Swedish Embassy with only a backpack and a pistol, and with something unique in the armory of a diplomat: an agreement from his foreign office to an extraordinary list of conditions. Wallenberg had insisted upon: appointment as first secretary; a free hand to use any methods he saw fit, including bribery; the authority to deal directly with anyone, including the prime minister, or his country's enemies; access to more funds, if needed, to be raised by a propaganda campaign in Sweden; and the permission to give asylum in any legation buildings to persons holding Swedish protective passports.

He immediately set about redesigning the Swedish protective passport so that it would impress the Nazis and their Hungarian counterparts. He established soup kitchens, hospitals, orphanages, and schools. He bought food on the black market to feed the rescued Jews in safe houses. Hundreds of volunteers suddenly became Swedish "diplomats" and thousands of Jews found themselves "Swedish" and taken under protection, and the original Swedish Legation members began adopting Wallenberg's methods. Using his authority, diplomatic and moral, Wallenberg confronted Nazi leaders, including Eichmann, intervened to rescue Jews from trains and forced marches, and finally, in one night, managed to instill in the mind of a German general such a fear of post-war retribution that 70,000 lives were saved when the general disobeyed orders to burn the Jewish ghetto.

What happened to Wallenberg at the end of the war remains a mystery. He was taken into the protective custody of the Russians on 17 January 1945 and was never seen again. In 1957 the then Deputy Foreign Minister Andrei Gromyko informed the government of Sweden that Wallenberg had died of a heart attack in 1947. But there have since been several reports of his having been seen alive. This Honorary Citizen of the United States, as he was named in 1981, has been the subject of talks between Reagan and Gorbachev, and others in their dealing with the Soviets.

In Per Anger's mind there is a chance that Wallenberg is still alive and he wants continued pressure on the Soviets to obtain his release. But whether dead or alive, Wallenberg should be held up, he believes, particularly for the younger generation, as an example of what one person can accomplish in a troubled world. As Elie Wiesel says, "Wallenberg will forever testify for man's need to remain human and his ability to succeed. That is why we wish to see him free, so as to thank him, thank him for enabling us, through his work and sacrifice, to proclaim our faith in human solidarity."

23 JUNE 1988

Painting donkeys and priests

LET ME TELL you an unusual newspaper story. It is about a cartoonist who in the 1960s was a household name in Britain and why he suddenly without fanfare faded from the scene. I refer to the inimitable Papas, who was illustrator and political cartoonist for *The Guardian*, and also drew for *Punch*, and the *Sunday Times*.

One afternoon, as *The Guardian* editorial staff were preparing the next day's edition, their colleague Bill Papas emerged from the men's washroom practically naked. Luckily a friend intercepted him and shepherded him back to where his clothes were. "When you start walking around the area in the nude," says Papas, "you must have had it. My end had come."

After 12 years of political cartooning, begun with a passion to change the world, 12 years of using humor to be vicious, of "ranting and raving and making huge statements that nobody heard," he was drinking a bottle of scotch a day and had ulcers and headaches, he was banned from his country of birth, South Africa, and from Eastern Europe, and his cartoons could not be published in his father's country, Greece. Two of his political cartoonist friends had committed suicide. "You can become mental," he says.

Papas told his editor, Alastair Hetherington, that he would

like to resign. Hetherington said, "Why don't you take a year's sabbatical. You need it." So a new life began for the cartoonist. And England's loss has, with the passage of time, become America's gain. For Papas, and his English artist wife, Tessa, are now widely acclaimed for their sketching and painting of scenes in the United States, and have opened the Chetwynd Stapylton Gallery in Portland, where they now live.

William Papas was born in Ermelo, South Africa, in 1927. His first language was Swazi, followed by Afrikaans, then English, French, German, Swedish, languages he picked up when he travelled as a young man. But his effective language has always been drawing. In fact, his book about how to speak Greek, which is principally sketches, has been a best seller in that country, with 10,000 copies sold every year since 1972.

He had some formal artistic education at art schools in England, but his real training was the sketching he learned to do on street corners and byways as he waited for lifts hitchhiking around Europe.

Given a year off on full pay, Papas opted for Greece and returned to his father's village. He and Tessa enjoyed the sun, the village life, the boat trips, and the sketching and painting without deadlines and pressure. A year later, the call to return to *The Guardian* forced him to make a clean break with the past. He found that the same stories, the same things were happening in London as when he left, and he just couldn't face going back to his old job.

So began 14 years of "retirement," of what some might feel was an idyllic life, with 6 months of sailing on a yacht, then months of life in a cottage, sketching and painting. He developed his exaggerated, semi-abstract style, combining humor and affection. Out of that time came, too, a book on Jerusalem that sold 30,000 copies. "But I became terribly, terribly bored," he says. Tessa adds, "One beautiful bay after another and you can't paint donkeys and priests forever."

With the whole world to choose from, the 63-year-old artist

says that America was the last place where he ever thought of settling. But exhibitions in Chicago and Scottsdale brought the couple here. For 2½ years they travelled 100,000 miles around the United States by car, producing *Papas' America*, which sold 700 copies at $500 to $1000 each. Tessa, who wrote the accompanying text, describes the sketchbook as "an open invitation to people to sit down and talk and share their stories."

Nowhere they went attracted them more than Portland, Oregon. They liked the city the moment they saw it. "After fifteen years of sunshine, I like rain," he jokes. Every week the Portland *Downtowner* runs one of Papas's sketches of the city. "The best thing is the historic value, not the artistic value," he says modestly. (Many of the landmarks he has drawn have already been demolished.) He is also painting vivid, colorful, swirling pictures of horses, a favorite subject since he was a child. Some impressive ones are on display in the gallery.

Tessa finds herself drawn to the scenery of eastern and central Oregon, for she likes to do landscapes—"the starker the better." Papas may have won his first art prize at the age of 7 but he can never emulate Tessa in one achievement. She had a painting exhibited in the Royal Academy when she was 12. It was a fox-hunting scene. The Chetwynd Stapylton Gallery is named after Tessa's grandmother, a very spirited lady who lived to be 100.

Papas has not lost his appreciation of good cartooning and regularly schedules showings of the best in this country and Britain. But he is more skeptical nowadays of their effect. He likes to show the drawings of his predecessor at *The Guardian*, Low, who in 1935–1936 portrayed Hitler, predicting what he would be like and what he would do and imploring Britain to rearm. Papas' own drawings from the 1960s are often a preview of events that would be repeated in one way or another 20 years later.

Sometimes he regrets his decision to leave *The Guardian*.

But he claims there is a lethargy in London now that he contrasts with the dynamism he feels in Portland. He promises he won't do any political cartooning here. "I like Portland too much to be thrown out of it," he says.

23 AUGUST 1990

Parachute perspective

FLIGHT LIEUTENANT David Howell, a holder of Britain's Distinguished Flying Cross, who flew as a navigator on bombing raids over Germany, wrote me recently, "I am thankful that so much rebuilding and rebirth has been possible in a country which I and others helped to destroy. I feel nothing but a real kinship with today's Germany."

The Scottish airman, a devout Christian, is one of those former enemies who helped to lay some of the foundations for a democratic Germany.

As World War II drew to a close and Howell was on his twenty-third sortie, the wings of his Lancaster bomber iced up and the plane went into a steep dive. Only the combined effort of pilot and flight engineer managed to level the plane at 4000 feet, long enough for the crew to jump.

Fear had often assailed Howell on these raids and a first jump into thick cloud was no exception. "But I had learned to face fear and hand it over to God," he says. "It was a perfect moment for God to take over." After the first jerk of the parachute's opening he remembers the sensation as pleasant. He thought of his mother who would receive a telegram that he was missing and he prayed for her. He thought of his friends who had introduced him to the discipline of regular moments of quiet to listen for God's guidance. This was such a moment, he thought.

As the clouds broke and he saw the Rhine he felt that he had something to give his enemies, that "we were meant," as he puts it, "to fight together for a new world."

Taken for interrogation, he found himself before an English-speaking officer who admitted that the war would soon be over, that Germany had lost. "What do you think will happen to my country?" he asked. Howell replied, "What I feel my country needs, and yours, too, is a new spirit based on doing what is right, running things the way God shows."

"That is the first time I have heard that answer given," said the interrogator. "Please tell me more."

So the POW told the German officer how he and others had made a new start by measuring their lives against absolute moral standards and putting right the things that were wrong. "These standards are like a beam you can always fly along," he said.

"Let us continue in the morning," said the German.

Howell asked for pencil and paper, and during the night wrote at length what he saw for a new Germany after the war. He gave it to the interrogator. "Thank you," he said. "My name is von Schilling."

Nine years later Howell was in Mannheim. He had often wondered what became of von Schilling. By chance, he discovered that he was the editor of the *Mannheimer Morgen*, the city's main paper, and they met. The German editor had never forgotten the earlier conversation and, indeed, had even used his paper to present some of Howell's ideas.

The two have remained friends. Just before writing me Howell had phoned the editor, now retired, to congratulate him on the reunification of Germany. "The bridge built in 1945," says Howell, "remains strong."

I was told this story first by Howell. But I also heard about it from von Schilling in his Mannheim newspaper office.

9 OCTOBER 1990

Maori peacemaker

GERMAN FIELD MARSHAL Erwin Rommel once said, "Give me the Maori battalion and I will conquer the world." He was speaking of the courage of the World War II army unit drawn from the native people of New Zealand. Like the Gurkhas of Nepal, the Maoris have established a fearsome reputation on the battlefield. It has also spilled over onto the playing field. The famous New Zealand rugby team, the All Blacks, like many New Zealand teams, start their games with a *haka*, a Maori war dance, designed to make foes tremble.

Perhaps the most famous World War II battle in which the Maori battalion participated was at Monte Cassino in Italy. The chaplain to the battalion, whose bravery in that battle won him one of Britain's highest decorations, the Military Cross, is Canon Wi Te Tau Huata. The citation spoke of his indifference to enemy fire as he brought in the wounded.

Son and grandson of Anglican priests, Canon Huata is chaplain to the Maori Queen, Te Atairangikaahu. He believes his people are meant to be the peacemakers of the Pacific, as he told a nationwide audience on Radio New Zealand. The year 1990 is crucial for relations between the white population, known as *pakehas*, and the Polynesian Maoris. For it is the 150th anniversary of the Treaty of Waitangi, signed by the whites with the Maoris but not ratified and, according to many whites and most Maoris, not fully honored.

Canon Huata is a bridge builder. At the 1989 Waitangi Day celebrations he was asked both by a group of young Maori radicals and by chiefs and elders to conduct services. He used the occasions to challenge both. To the chiefs and elders he said, "Don't forget that our Lord had the toughest things to say to the Pharisees, not to the sinners. Watch out for self-righteousness when you judge the young radicals." To the radicals who had been preaching racism, hatred, and violence, he said, "Your desire to redress the injustices of the path is on the right track. But your strategy is wrong and even evil. You speak of lands confiscated by the Crown. Don't forget that our tribes confiscated land from each other. Let us build on that Treaty unless you have something better to put in its place."

As the Canon told an earlier conference at Waikenae, "When the Maori takes a slab of wood he carves the right side first and then carves the left to balance this. The Maori and the pakeha balance each other in their characteristics. The pakeha's strong point is his individuality, to stand up for what is right. We Maoris have a great gift in our ability to work together and in our sense of communion with each other. The pakeha is best at the long distance while the Maori is best in the short sprint. We must use these gifts for the Pacific."

The Canon's honesty and fearlessness draws on his character. After one particularly frightening wartime battle he decided to tell his troops at a battalion church parade that he had been so fearful that he'd been tempted to quit. Sermons were normally in the Maori language. But on this occasion they were joined by Field Marshal Alexander, the supreme commander, and General Freyberg, the head of the New Zealand contingent. He decided to say in English what he had already in mind. Afterwards, General Freyberg said, "That was the most courageous sermon I've heard. I understand very well how you felt. I was scared to death before the action that produced my Victoria Cross (British medal of honor)."

The Canon's effectiveness also flows, however, from an answer to what he calls "a cancer of bitterness," his prejudice against Catholics when his son married one and to his hatred of his wartime enemy, the Germans. "Unity with my family and unity with former enemies followed when I put right what I had done wrong," he says. "While I held bitterness I was blind to the needs of our own family."

In 1971, on his way to the Moral Re-Armament conference in Caux, Switzerland, he had flown over Italy and the pilot of his plane, unaware of its significance to him, had pointed out Monte Cassino below. It reminded the Canon that in the war he had prayed that Germany would be destroyed. At Caux he was moved when a German woman said she was sorry for her people's treatment of the Jews. The two experiences were a challenge, he felt, to practise what he preached. "By honestly accepting blame and asking forgiveness," he said, "she made me see that hate and faith could not exist side by side in the same heart."

At the conference he made friends with the nephew of General Westphal, Rommel's successor as commander of the Afrika Corps. As a result a contingent from the Maori Battalion was sent an invitation to the Afrika Corps reunion. Canon Huata read the invitation to veterans assembled at a cathedral service before their own reunion in New Zealand. He told them this story of what happened to him.

Twenty-six Maoris responded—and were given a tumultuous welcome by the 7000 Afrika Corps veterans. The Canon was seated beside Frau Rommel and her son, Manfred, and asked to speak. "This is a time for brotherhood," he said. "A time for reconciliation. A time for forgiveness. A time for cleansing. We cannot spell 'forgiving' without spelling 'giving.' We cannot spell 'brothers' without 'others.' We cannot spell 'communion' without spelling 'union.'" General Westphal responded, "Your greatness is not only in battle but also in your hearts by accepting our invitation of goodwill. You are the peacemakers."

Canon Huata likes to quote the words of another Afrika Corps veteran when he saw Huata's broad girth, "We must have been lousy shots to miss you!" As New Zealand approaches this crucial year many will be grateful that they did.

22 JUNE 1989

Crazy prime minister

A white man looks at a black man as an inferior.
But you put a gun in your hand,
Then a white man will respect you in your own country.

THESE ARE THE WORDS of a song, translated from the Russian, which Robert Gwavava and others sang when they were undergoing ideological training in Eastern Europe. "I was singing and creating the momentum for revenge," he says. "I never dreamt I could become a friend to my fellow white Zimbabweans," as the citizens of his independent African country are known.

I talked with Robert and his wife, Joyce, at the Moral Re-Armament conference center in Caux, Switzerland. His experiences should serve as a caution to those who too easily write off the nascent democracy of this southern African country, or who do not see beyond the media shorthand attached to its people and policies.

Robert's story is typical of many in his country's freedom struggle. In 1960 he was arrested for public violence. "I was using petrol bombs to destroy white humanity," he said. He spent 3 years in prison, at one point coughing up blood from beatings he received. Released, he became secretary-general of the Rhodesian Tailors and Garment Workers Union, representing them at conferences abroad. This was a cover as, unknown to the authorities, he had a British passport as well as his Rhodesian one. He would use Botswana as an exit and then fly to Lusaka, Zambia, and cities in Europe to link up with the liberation struggle. When the authorities found him out and tried to make him take bribes and endangered his life, he skipped off to Botswana on his way to a conference of the Organization of African Trade Union Unity in Libya, and then back to Lusaka. He was then sent to Romania for training in Marxism and Leninism, followed by further studies in Marxist philosophy in Moscow, returning home from there shortly before independence.

Returning to Zimbabwe, Gwavava was aghast to find his new prime minister, Robert Mugabe, calling for reconciliation rather than revenge. "We thought he was crazy." Gwavava was not ready for this challenge. When he left Rhodesia he had been a lay preacher, but the humiliation, the imprisonment, the beatings, and the 7-year separation from his family, had made him a slave of hatred. At independence he had taken a job as a labor relations officer so he could get his own back at white employers. But, as he says, the grace of God, backed by the prayers of his family, was preparing him for change.

"I was ruthless and wretched," he says, "drinking and going round with women." An experience in church made him realize the need to do away with the beer and drop some of his friends. "All of a sudden God filled my life. God was speaking to me. I began to love, I started to trust, I learned to apologize, to forgive." And as he changed he recognized the wisdom of Mugabe's approach, that it saved the country from further civil war. "It showed a kind of heart that recognized the will of God," he says, "because it took into account the power of forgiveness."

Gwavava is impressed by the way the prime minister has included the churches in the task of nation-building. Political changes, he believes, are coming as a result of consultation and consent, not imposed from above. Zimbabwe would not be a carbon copy of any other country. Zimbabwe's positive approach to the problems of racial and tribal differences, and its integration of rival armies with differing allegiances, are, he believes, an example for South Africa. "Change performs wonders in nation-building," he told me. "Through change, Zimbabwe is now a unified nation with a single leadership."

Gwavava's own approach has been different since. At the Ministry of Labor he became known as a reconciler. And, now with the National Employment Council, he continues to work for cooperation. He no longer sees color as the issue and is, as he says, singing a different song.

2 SEPTEMBER 1988

One act of madness

RATU MELI VESIKULA radiates the self assurance that comes from being born to a chief's family in Fiji and attaining the rank of regimental sergeant major in the British Army. But he is now, he tells me, in a phase of change and healing in his life, an experience he would like his country to share. I met him recently at an international conference in Switzerland.

"Fiji—the way the world should be" was the proud boast of the island's tourist brochures. Until 1987 that is, when, in what he calls "one act of madness," the harmony of the two main races, native Fijians and Indians, was shattered by a coup.

The Fijian chief loves his country. It is what brought him home after 23 years service in the British Army, service for which he was decorated by the Queen. He recognized quickly the need for changes in Fijian society but expected that these would be achieved by the normal parliamentary process, not through the barrel of a gun.

The coup had been proclaimed "in the name of the indigenous people" and soon Ratu Meli was enlisted to lead a nationalist movement with the slogan "Fiji for the Fijians." "I advocated violence, instigated violence, talked of sending Indians away from Fiji," he says. "I was in the thick of things."

It took him 4 or 5 months to realize that the coup was not

after all undertaken for the benefit of the indigenous people. For the chief this new realization was a time of "personal revolution," which led to his apologizing to the Indian people through the English and Hindi press for the way he had treated them. "They were victimized and made scapegoats," he says. It also led to his being persecuted, jailed, sued, and labeled a betrayer of his people.

His new awareness about what had been happening gripped him so tight, he says, that he wanted to take on singlehandedly those he claims led his country astray. "But I am learning to forgive. I'm finding it hard. I am looking forward to the opportunity to approach them, to say 'sorry' for my hatred." He is initiating a conference in Fiji to try to bring people of different views together and to recommence a dialogue that has been lacking since the coup.

"I only hope God will one day open the door so that we can go forward as one nation," he says. He has announced his withdrawal from political activity to concentrate on working with the poor people of Fiji. His passion: to see restored the harmony between races that Pope John Paul II praised on his visit to Fiji.

4 SEPTEMBER 1990

Dangerous to evil

"So LONG AS there are people like Victor Sparre in the world," wrote Soviet dissident Vladimir Maximov, "those suffering oppression need not feel they are alone."

Victor Sparre is one of Norway's leading artists, best known for his stained-glass windows. But he is also what he calls a "committed artist" seeking to defend the right of individuals to be themselves. That is why, he says, he will so often paint a clown whose only sin is to be different, to think otherwise, in a regimented and bureaucratic world.

He is a committed person of faith, too, who takes as a guide the words of a great Finnish artist, Lennart Segerstraale, who once said, "We must create an art which is dangerous to evil."

"We artists," Sparre wrote in his book *The Flame in the Darkness*, "are a chosen group in today's world. To us has been vouchsafed a power that can set men free. Art may be the last defence of the individual against the colossal forces that seek to make us conform."

Twelve years ago he wrote that in the Soviet Union it seemed as if Art alone were left to resist tyranny, with writers posing a more deadly threat to the regime than terrorists: "When a weapon is smuggled into a camp to a Russian freedom fighter, it will be, not a gun, but a novel or a book of poems."

Over the years Sparre befriended many Soviet dissidents, making several visits to the Soviet Union. He was the first person Solzhenitsyn sought out when he came to the West in 1974 and when he considered settling in Norway. Sparre was a close friend of Sakharov; it was in Sakharov's home that Maximov first met the Norwegian artist.

Last month another Norwegian artist, the pianist Kjell Baekkelund, wrote in a report from Moscow for the Oslo daily, *Aftenposten*, "It must be strange to be Victor Sparre these days: for more than 20 years he was refused permission to enter the Soviet Union. He was undesirable. Both on account of his courageous opinions and because of his friendship with Sakharov and Solzhenitsyn. And now, today, he is feted to the skies in Moscow, where a retrospective exhibition of forty-five of his pictures, from 1948 to 1990, is being given in the gallery of the Moscow Artists' Federation."

Some 150,000 people saw the Sparre exhibition in its first week and it had to be extended a further week. Before its opening the Norwegian Ambassador to the Soviet Union, Dagfinn

Stenseth, gave a lunch in the artist's honor, which was attended by personalities from Soviet art, music, and literature.

The exhibition has a magnificent catalog in Russian with a foreword by Norwegian Foreign Minister Thorvald Stoltenberg, in which he stresses Sparre's contribution to humanity and his absolute loyalty to honesty in his writing and speaking.

Victor Sparre ended his book *The Flame in the Darkness*, "I believe that the Russian dissidents' lesson to mankind is that we must all be ourselves first and so gain the freedom to create beyond ourselves. No one of us, neither they nor I, has found the answer to every question, but we have set our feet on the path because, each in our own way, we have become dissidents to the outdated doctrines of society, have allowed ourselves to be stripped of materialist values and are free, if we will, to be guided by our consciences and the Holy Spirit within us.

"He who has found inner freedom and become a flame in the darkness has won the greatest victory a man can win, not only for himself but for all humanity. Wherever it happens it brings joy and power."

11 APRIL 1991

Buried alive

IT WAS AN EXTREME example of bad things happening to good people. It was also a demonstration of how God can put bad things to good use. At least that's how I think the author might characterize the central event of her startling book, *Beyond Violence*.

It is a ray of hope out of an increasingly violent South Africa to hear the story of a white woman, Agnes Leakey Hofmeyr, and her husband, Bremer, who with every good reason to seek revenge or withdraw in bitterness, have devoted their lives to better race relations, pioneering interracial exchanges and conferences long before it became normal, earning the enmity of the Broederbond and, as the book records, the frontal disapproval of Prime Minister Verwoerd.

Agnes Hofmeyr feels that in South Africa today the stakes are so high that nothing should be withheld "if it might in any way help the estranged peoples of our country to find one another in a new South Africa."

Gray Leakey, Agnes' father, was, indeed, a good man. He first came to Kenya from Britain in 1908 to help his uncle, father of the anthropologist Louis Leakey, to build a mission church and school. Gray had been a typical settler but one day decided to apologize to his African workers for the times he had hurt them through his anger and to tell them of his decision to run his farm not just for profit but for the good of all and for the good of the country. As Agnes writes, the name he had been given earlier by Africans, Morungaru, meaning straight and tall, took on the added meaning of being upright.

In the 1950s the Mau Mau movement was active in Kenya. Unlike many settlers Gray refused to carry a gun. As the fortunes of Mau Mau waned a prophetess of the Mau Mau claimed it was because the gods were angry. They had to be placated by a human sacrifice. And it had to be of a good man. They chose Gray.

Sixty Mau Mau attacked the family home, killed Agnes' stepmother and the cook, and bound her father hand and foot and dragged him up Mount Kenya. He talked to them in Kikuyu about the things that had to change in the country and told them that killing people would not bring the changes needed or a happy country. They buried him alive. The news was sent to Agnes by a Kikuyu chief whose own father had been murdered by the Mau Mau.

For Agnes, who had been working tirelessly for racial harmony, this was a shattering blow. The death of her father came close to being the death of her commitment. But as she took time to reflect she had the insistent thought, "Have no bitterness or hatred but fight harder than ever to bring a change of heart to black and white alike."

She went further. As she and Bremer reflected on their traditions they realized that although they had tried to be good they had taken for granted the colonial structure. Another strong thought came to Agnes, "You must be responsible for the sins of your race, just as you are responsible for your own wrongs."

Many years later, after she had faithfully fulfilled that mandate of "no bitterness or hatred" and her story had been used to give hope to many, she received an apology from one who had been on the committee that had plotted her father's murder. Events had come full circle, for this man had just been one of a committee that had been working to elect another of her family, Philip Leakey, to parliament.

The startling thing in this book is that Agnes goes beyond forgiving those who planned and carried out her father's murder. This is spelled out in the book's concluding paragraph, "We whites were very conscious of the good things we had done. The blacks were very conscious of the bad things we had done. We people are more conscious of where we have been hurt than where we have hurt others. I had to identify with the wrong things we whites had done and realize that I stood in need of forgiveness, and I did ask the Kikuyu for forgiveness. So perhaps a key to the question, 'How can I forgive?' is to look at another question, 'How much do I need forgiveness?'"

The story of her father's death is but one episode in a rich tapestry. There are wonderful descriptions of growing up in the wilds, living in tents, transported by ox-drawn carts, watching out for lions, looking after Louis Leakey's animals when he went to Cambridge. Shoes were worn once a week— for church. This "colonial" existence is in contrast to being sent back to what seemed a constricted English education, and then a religious experience that led to a reconciliation with her father (who had married again after her mother had died suddenly), and that took her and her husband to many continents.

I can understand why South African writer Derek Gill, author of *The Dove* and other books and now living in California, believes some of the events she describes "are assuredly substance for another box-office hit on colonial Africa." The book gives a glimpse into a remarkable family: her older brother won posthumously Britain's highest decoration for valor, the Victoria Cross, another brother became a general.

Beyond Violence reminds me of *The Flame Trees of Thika* and *Out of Africa* though it is less centered on a past that has gone forever than on a future that could be. As the Johannesburg *Star* writes, *Beyond Violence* is superbly titled. It is a story of hurt, hate—and profoundly moving faith and hope."

13 DECEMBER 1990

7 Working it out

A STORY DEALING with a problem or tragedy should at least report the basic changes of action or thought required to deal constructively with a current situation or to prevent a similar problem in the future. Thus, a reporter needs to be expectantly alert to finding sources who are bringing a constructive approach to any given problem.

> From guidelines used by radio and TV staff
> of the *Christian Science Monitor*

Indian flood

THE UNITED STATES can take a little credit for the award this week of the World Food Prize to Dr. Verghese Kurien, chairman of India's National Dairy Development Board. More than 40 years ago Dr. Kurien won a scholarship to study dairy science at Michigan State University. After receiving his Master of Science of Mechanical Engineering (with distinction) in 1949, he was assigned to work with an Indian government experimental dairy in Anand, Gujarat.

At a ceremony at the Smithsonian Institution this week Kurien will be honored for his work to produce and market milk throughout India. Involving 6 million dairy producers in 50,000 cooperatives and marketing 3 million tons of milk annually to 500 cities and towns, "Operation Flood," as it is called, is the largest agricultural development program in the world. Kurien calls it "the white revolution." It all stems from his years of commitment to that Anand dairy.

The $200,000 World Food Prize was established by the General Foods Fund in 1986 on the initiative of Dr. Norman E. Borlaug, who won the 1970 Nobel Peace Prize for his contributions to the "green revolution." Borlaug wanted to see a comparable award set up to honor individual contributions to the addressing and alleviating of hunger and malnutrition. He is now chairman of the selection committee for the World Food Prize and believes Kurien's work has the elements needed to improve the quality and quantity of the world's food supply —effective production, processing, and distribution.

Most of the milk producers who participate in Operation Flood are small farmers, with two thirds owning only one or two cows or buffaloes. Nearly a quarter of the participants are landless. The cooperative provides these milk producers with animal feed, veterinary services, and artificial insemination. And perhaps most important, the farmers receive immediate payment, at steady prices, for their milk—and the public is assured a stable supply of safe milk.

To enroll in a village cooperative, a producer must pay 1 rupee (about 8 cents) and purchase at least one 10-rupee share. Each cooperative is run by a locally elected committee, and the cooperatives own the district unions. "The dairies are managed by the employees of the farmers," says Kurien, "not bureaucrats deputed by the government."

The United Nations Food and Agricultural Organization attributes the success of Operation Flood to, among other things, the participation of "honest, dedicated, and motivated social workers of the Gandhian tradition," the design of by-laws to "discourage vested interest," and effective management and audits, which "keep the entire structure free from corruption and scandal."

India's milk production has doubled in the last 20 years, according to Minister of Agriculture Bhajan Lal, and the country aims to produce 46 million tons of milk this year and 64 million by 1994. Since 1976 there have been no commercial imports of dairy products (except some special cheeses) and dairy food aid accounts for less than 1 percent of the country's milk production. All milk products found in the shops of India are now produced in India from Indian milk.

In India Kurien's principles have been adopted in other fields, too, including an electrical cooperative for an area with a population of more than 3 million, an infrastructure for the production, purchase, processing, and marketing of oil seeds and vegetable oil, and the largest and most technologically advanced cold storage and fruit and vegetable handling facility in the country.

The success of Operation Flood is also having a significant social effect on Indian society. By treating all members of their cooperative equally, and including the *harijans*, the former un-touchables, Operation Flood has helped break down the country's caste barriers. For true development, says Kurien, is the development of people, not of cows, and can only happen as people are given responsibility for managing their own affairs.

19 OCTOBER 1989

Cornflakes and corruption

I WAS AWAKENED at 5 o'clock each morning recently by the call to prayer from the minaret nearest us in the northern Nigerian city of Jos. "God is great. God is great. There is no other God but the one true God. Let's go for prayer," came the words of the muezzin, which, in a concession to modernity, were not shouted over the rooftops but spoken into a microphone and broadcast through loudspeakers.

"Prayer is more important than sleep," the faithful are reminded, and by the second call, at 5:30, my host, Osman, a devout Muslim, was out of bed for the first of his five daily observances of prayer. "Sometimes," he admits, "the devil presses me down on the bed. But I say, 'I seek refuge in Allah from Satan' and then I jump up."

Forty-five-year-old Osman Ibrahim Shum is an Ethiopian, from Eritrea, who has lived 12 years in Nigeria and is the manager of the country's largest biscuit company. "The king of biscuits—everything other biscuits are trying to be" is their advertising slogan. At its height the company was producing 1200 tons of biscuits a month. But because of foreign exchange difficulties the government banned wheat imports from America and a program for growing wheat locally had to be started. Now the company's 850 workers produce 650 tons a month.

The Nigerian military government, which is promoting self-reliance and pride in the consumption of home-produced commodities, is trying to create a new cultural environment that includes the elimination of corruption and dishonesty. Osman is one of those whose practical example may be more effective than slogans.

When Osman first arrived in Nigeria his job was to clear imported materials through the port of Apapa. He prepared his first bill of lading, describing the value and quantity of goods and giving the appropriate tariff number. A customs officer suggested he should use a different tariff number, which would mean less duty would have to be paid. The money saved, he was told, would be divided three ways between him, the customs officer, and the officer's colleagues. "I had heard about corruption," Osman told me, "but I didn't know it was so openly discussed as if it was a normal business transaction. That shocked me." Because of his refusal to cooperate he found that his papers were not always attended to promptly and he had to pay demurrage for goods that had not been cleared. At that point a task force was chasing importers to clear goods and many calculated whether the bribe or the demurrage would be more expensive. "That was their basis for choice," he says. "Mine was whether it was right or wrong."

It was difficult for him also with his staff, some of whom were involved in the practice. "A company that approves of this sort of thing," he says, "then has no idea whether the man who says he needs a certain sum of money to clear a certain consignment actually uses that much or not. If you go along with it," he says, "your clerk will only do to you what you are doing to government. You lose authority. You can't dismiss him." Osman doesn't claim that he always succeeded in his 2½ years at the port. Sometimes it was easier to turn a blind eye. But he was determined not to become part of what he calls "a sickness." "If more people did that," he says, "it would begin to change things."

In his present position he has tried to hold the same line with the result that his company is regarded as a model for sound management. He is grateful for the backing of the owner of the company in a policy of no bribes and a straightforward job.

Since he joined the company in 1983 the correct excise duty has been paid and customs officers, despite their complaints, have not been given a cent for favors or for bending any rules.

In January this year Osman had a fresh challenge. There was a new customs officer who didn't know what Osman stood for. The government had just abolished excise duty on most of his company's products, like biscuits and bread, but not on cornflakes. The officer suggested that he write a letter thanking the government and saying that this should also apply to cornflakes and until the matter was clarified he wouldn't pay the duty. The officer would forward the letter and the company would not have to pay for at least a year. Don't bother about me, he explained, he was a friend but he had some expenses taking care of others in the town and in the capital. "I just laughed," says Osman. "I told him, 'We can't do that. I'm already grateful for what the government has done. I won't cheat them. Cornflakes is roasted cereal and it is clear that the exemption is not for us.' He must have thought I was stupid."

Osman says that his attitudes in business go back to a decision made many years ago to take his Muslim faith seriously and to make restitution for equipment he had stolen from a basketball team in Asmara that he managed. "Bribery is forbidden in Islam," he says. "You are forbidden to give or take. It is a great sin. I saw that unless I cleaned up my own life I couldn't do anything in my country."

When you are engaged in bribery, he told me, you lose your freedom and are controlled by the fear that things may get out. "You can't talk with authority about corruption because every time you talk you remember things you have done."

Osman likes to quote a saying of the Prophet: "Take wisdom wherever you find it; no harm which source it comes from."

I think non-Muslims might find wisdom and encouragement in the way Osman has gone about his work.

15 MARCH 1990

A cry for help

IT MAY BE that, in a sense, we are all responsible for a crisis like the environmental disaster in Prince William Sound, Alaska. I was interested in the perspective of Malcolm Roberts, who is executive director of Commonwealth North, a 400-member organization of Alaskan leaders who study issues affecting the future of their state.

In an article in the international magazine *For a Change* he says that most of the lessons of the oil spill won't be known for a long time. After an oil spill, time is the enemy and speedy action is needed, and we still have a lot to learn about which clean-up measures help and which hurt. But the most important lesson, in his view, is that the actions of the individual still count. "Industries, states, even nations can depend," he writes, "on one tanker captain, one railroad engineer, one airline mechanic, one person in charge of a nuclear silo."

When the captain of the ill-fated *Exxon Valdez*, who had admitted his alcohol problems to his employer years earlier, was asked shortly after his ship hit the reef what he thought the problem was, he replied, "I think you're looking at it."

"Someone wasn't listening when he asked for help," says Roberts, "or if they were, they didn't follow up. This," he concludes, "is the cardinal message learned to date from the great Alaska oil spill. When one of our fellow human beings gives a cry for help, we'd best respond. A world could depend on it."

Of course, an individual can steer a wrong course, or help a company chart a right one. With all the recriminations that fly around about Exxon and its failures I have just received encouraging news about another multi-national corporation, Broken Hill Proprietary (BHP), Australia's largest company in steel, mining, and oil.

Tom Ramsay, whom I first met some 30 years ago when he

was a young industrial chemist with Shell Oil, decided that absolute honesty would be a standard in his work in industry. Over the years he worked his way up to planning manager of BHP's oil and gas division.

When BHP discovered the oil field in the Bass Strait, Ramsay says, they worked out a way to calculate the crude oil price to which government and industry agreed. For the first year BHP had to rely on the oil analysis of another company. When BHP set up their own analysis their figures came out differently, and if accepted would mean a drop in the price of crude.

Tom Ramsay had the job of recommending a course of action to management. After 6 months of debate a letter was drafted that would have perpetuated the wrong method. He showed it to his wife. Without understanding the technical details her reaction was that the letter was devious. This rang a bell with him. He went back to his boss who said, "Yes, you're right, it is devious."

Eventually Ramsay was called in to see the managing director, Sir James McNeil, to explain the issues. When he did a senior manager pointed out that putting the mistake right would cost the company $10 million over the next 5 years. Sir James looked at him over the top of his glasses. "I'm more interested in the good name of BHP than in ten million dollars," he said. Not only did he then agree to the action that would lose $10 million but insisted that customers who had been inadvertently overcharged should get a refund.

Tom Ramsay was given the job of handing over checks totalling $1.1 million each. A friend of Ramsay in another company said to him afterwards, "We could never understand why you raised this—we realized it was going to cost you money. But now I think it is worth every cent because of the trust that's been created between us."

6 JUNE 1989

Leaving the past behind

PRESIDENT BUSH will represent the United States at the State funeral of Emperor Hirohito of Japan. The Duke of Edinburgh will be there for Britain. I am glad they will be, despite criticism in both countries by those who regard the emperor as a war criminal. It is an advantage that they are themselves veterans of World War II.

I recently had a visitor, Robert Angel, who is knowledgeable about Japan. He speaks the language, has lived and taught there, and was president of the Japan Economic Institute in Washington, D.C. Three things, he said, came to his mind at this time. One, that the feeling in Japan about the death of the emperor, although expected, is probably stronger than the feelings Americans had when President Kennedy was shot. Two, that the Japanese are far more sensitive about their monarchy than we realize. "They can make jokes about it, we can't," he said. "They can criticize but it is not appreciated when foreigners do." And three, "What America says and does at this time will be remembered."

That, of course, applies to Britain as well. So I was upset at the intemperate words used by some British papers about the emperor which were then, of course, picked up by the Japanese press. I was glad that an English friend of mine, who was a soldier in the Asian theater in World War II and was decorated for his bravery, spoke up about this at an international conference in Korea. He called the press statements "insulting and untrue" and apologized to the Japanese who were present, assuring them that the press did not represent the views of the majority of the British people.

Terrible things were done during the war. And there are people still alive who suffered from them and still do. The reactions of those who have never got beyond their bitterness are understandable. But as a letter in the London daily *Inde-*

pendent from four British ex-servicemen states, "It is not possible to forget, but we have found it possible to forgive. We have seen the power of apology and forgiveness by individuals to break the chain of hate, which otherwise continues to each succeeding generation."

With hindsight it is possible to debate whether the emperor could have done more to prevent war, though it is difficult to see how. He was kept even more remote from events than the last Chinese emperor. But his distaste for Japanese imperialistic policies is well recorded, his actions to bring to an end the war, probably saving hundreds of thousands of Allied and Japanese lives, are part of history, as well as his willingness to take on himself the responsibility for his country's actions. It should also be noted that our representatives at the state funeral will be honoring an institution rather than an individual.

Japan over the years has gone far beyond what was expected in trying to make amends for the war. I was struck, as I was preparing this commentary, to read that when Hitachi began operations in a small Kentucky town, one of the first things its representatives did was to set up a meeting with survivors of the Bataan death march to explain how sorry they were and how they were from a different generation.

One of our big newspapers in Britain, the *Sunday Mirror*, had some wise words on the subject: "As a nation we cannot dwell in the past. Bitterness is an arid emotion. It has no harvest. That is why it is right for our royal family to be represented at the funeral of Emperor Hirohito. An insult would have been an empty gesture, deeply resented by the majority of Japanese people who bear no responsibility for the war.

"We won the last war. It is not necessary to keep on fighting it. If the victims of Pearl Harbor can send their newly elected president to Hirohito's funeral, we can send the husband of the Queen."

21 FEBRUARY 1990

I'm wrong, but . . .

WHOLE-HEARTED apologies are well received. They are good for the person who apologizes and further amicable relations in family or society as a whole. Apologies that have built-in reservations or are conditional on a response from others are sometimes counterproductive.

I noticed three recent apologies that come into this latter category.

"I'd be glad to apologize," said Los Angeles Police Chief Daryl Gates, "in spite of the fact that the victim is on parole and a convicted robber."

"My choice of the word 'sympathizer' was not a good one," said Senator Alan Simpson, referring to his criticism of Peter Arnett, "The word 'dupe' or 'tool' would have been more in context with my original comments."

"I'd like to apologize to all South Africans for any violence perpetrated by members of my party," said South African Inkatha leader Mangosuthu Buthelezi, but then added that apologies should also be forthcoming from the national executive of the African National Congress.

An apology is a chance to put something right, not a stick with which to beat someone else. That is why apologizing for the sins of your nation is best when you don't go on to say that it is somebody else's policy for which you are apologizing. Take these courageous words, for example, by a Japanese who was born after World War II. "I have made it a rule to apologize to Asian people whenever I meet them for what Japan did in the past," wrote Yukihisa Fujita in the *Japan Times* in March 1991. "As the fiftieth anniversary of Japan's sneak attack on Pearl Harbor falls this year, some symbolic occasion should be organized for the nation's leaders and people to clearly show the world their regret and demonstrate this change in concrete policy." Fujita says that facing past history squarely is the prerequisite for change, and Japan should take responsibility for its past and future.

I note that an article in *Izvestia* in Moscow recently made the same point. Dr. Alexei Kiva wrote, "Personally I think that the whole Soviet community must repent. Perhaps we should start with an honest appraisal of our country's past and present—and be shocked at the part we have played, whether willingly or unwillingly. This is how conscience and the civic spirit awaken, bringing with them free thought and love of freedom."

As I write we journalists are pretty much in the national doghouse. We never rate high in the public's esteem anyway. George Will writes, "Fortunately we who practice period journalism are not required by the code of our craft to live or die by predictions." True enough, though it is probably not a bad thing for the public to remind us from time to time of what we have said. Many columnists got it wrong about the Gulf War and it is encouraging to see some of them saying so. David Gergen, in an editorial in *US News and World Report*, said as much and evoked a positive response from the public. So did syndicated columnist Norman Lockman. "If anything has taken a worse beating than the Iraqis in the last month and a half," he writes, "it is conventional wisdom. Many of us who thought we knew what we were talking about, because we talked to people who thought they knew what they were talking about, put our money on the wrong set of ponies. If we had been at the track, we'd have had to hitchhike home."

Syndicated columnist William Raspberry makes his gracious admission with considerable humor. "Is it okay if I take a bit of perverse credit for the astounding victory of the u.s.-led alliance against Iraq's Saddam Hussein? It seems obvious to me, if to no one else, that President Bush developed his stunningly successful strategy by reading every recommendation of mine—and then by doing just the opposite."

9 APRIL 1991

The German character

A REUNITED GERMANY will be a boon, not a bane, to the world. In the 45 years since World War II the Federal Republic has been exemplary in its adherence to democratic processes and unique in its efforts to make amends to those who suffered. As Hella Pick, who fled the Nazis as a child and whose relatives died in concentration camps, wrote in *The Guardian*, "By almost any test applied to the country's political life, and the respect accorded to individual human rights, the Federal Republic must rank with the United States for high marks, probably above Britain." And now East Germany has officially acknowledged its responsibility for the Nazi past.

These statements will not erase the memories of those who suffered, of those for whom the German language or German uniforms evoke alarm, of those who are still caught in the stereotypes of war or who have been brought up on films with the bumbling Teuton or cruel Hun losing to the virtuous Allies. I understand, though am saddened, by the concentration camp survivor who, when the Berlin Wall came down, said, "They don't deserve such happiness." I understand, too, that Poles want to keep Russian soldiers on their soil until they are sure their borders are inviolable.

But I do not believe there is anything in the German character that makes them worse or better than the English or Americans or Israelis or Russians or anyone. I submit that those who cannot forgive are less than honest about the deep reaches of cruelty in all our natures and the less honorable episodes in the past of most nations.

If I were a German who had no share in World War II, indeed who was born long after it was over, a category that includes most Germans, I would be less gracious than some about the self-righteous attitude of many people abroad. I can appreciate the perspective of Peter Nonnenmacher, German correspondent in London of the *Frankfurter Rundschau*, who, after watching the rerun of World War II on British television screens, wrote, "Here we sit at our desks, waiting for the all-clear: waiting for the strangely popular shadows of war to lift gradually and to reveal once more the familiar, if complex, contours of peace." I agree with columnist Mike Royko who says it's time to let go old grudges against Germans. I agree, too, with former CBS correspondent Richard C. Hottelet who feels that "unwarranted suspicion is poison that the 1990s do not need."

The issue of the role of an expanded Germany in an expanded Europe is crucial. It is key, too, in how the Soviet Union will behave in the coming years. That is why I rejoice that the presidents of Germany and of Czechoslovakia are two of the most outstanding men in the affairs of the world. Although their roles may be more symbolic than powerful, they are setting a reassuring moral tone. German President Richard von Weizsaecker, whom *The Economist* calls "a transparently decent man" was 12 when Hitler came to power. In a speech at Bergen-Belsen, he said, "I know of no responsible West German politician, no matter what his age, who wants to disclaim his responsibility on account of his age." He is working for reconciliation between Germany and the peoples of eastern Europe.

Meanwhile Czech President Vaclav Havel has said, "The issue of Germany should be considered not as an obstacle but as a process which should be accelerated. And a unified Germany should become part of the whole European order." He has suggested that his country might apologize to the 3 million Germans who were expelled from their homes in 1939, and has even equated being anti-German with being anti-Semitic.

Last month the two presidents met in Prague 51 years to the day that Hitler marched into the Czech capital. Their meeting was to symbolize a new start. Both men recalled that there had been beneficial as well as negative aspects of the 1000 years of ties between Germans and Czechs. The days in which healthy patriotism was transformed into an unhealthy nationalism directed against one's neighbors were over, said von Weizsaecker. History cannot be rewritten, said Havel. But it could be handled in a human, compatible and understanding manner. As the Munich *Sueddeutscher Zeitung* wrote, "The two heads of state proved the point at the meeting in Prague Castle. The tenor of their speeches and the way in which they made them was enough to make one feel they marked a major change for the better."

I was reminded of an unpublicized event 55 years earlier when Baron Eugene von Teuber, German-speaking heir to some 10,000 acres in Czechoslovakia, visited the much-loved President Tomas Masaryk, to apologize for the failure of his race and class to support Czechoslovakia. "We stood aside in our bitter pride and resentment," he told Thomas's son, Jan, a post-war prime minister, "refusing the hand which our years of experience, of trial and error, might have made helpful. I have been reading carefully your father's matchless aims for our country. We know that they can never be fulfilled unless people like me and my kind accept the responsibility for dealing with corrosive emotions which divide German from Czech and Czech from Slovak. It is to healing these rifts that my wife and I have dedicated our lives."

The president was too ill to receive Eugene but his son went to his bedside to convey his words. When he came out he said, "He was very touched. He had tears in his eyes. He told me to thank you for bringing him hope. He said if only more Germans could feel as he does and our own people could learn to feel as those two do it would give strength to our republic, our democracy."

I have a feeling that Masaryk would have rejoiced at the meeting of Havel and von Weizsaecker, and the hope and the strength they bring to democracy in central Europe.

26 APRIL 1990

Throw the rascals out

"THROW THE rascals out." That was a catchphrase at the last election. It didn't work very well because the rascals were always somebody else's representatives, not ours. And our perception of rascaldom may be more a media-shaped figment of imagination than a sober assessment of public life.

A news story yesterday, however, sheds a different light on the whole issue. It appears that we have now located the real rascals—and they are us.

A book to be published next week claims that nine out of ten U.S. citizens lie regularly, that nearly a third of married Americans have had an affair, that for $10 million 7 percent of the public would kill a stranger, etcetera. So it doesn't, on the surface of things, look as if we have much of a leg to stand on in criticizing our representatives, whether they deserve it or not.

The book, *The Day America Told the Truth—What People Really Believe About Everything that Really Matters*, is based on the polling of some 6000 Americans about their attitudes on morality and religion. A wire service report says that the survey "produced a disturbing portrait of a nation without a common morality."

Now, I am very distrustful of the veracity of such polls or such books. The harm they do is to provide a salve to our consciences. If everybody's doing it, it can't be so bad, can it? I wouldn't be surprised if the public felt that they and their friends did not fit this new profile we are being offered. It must be someone else.

I would caution against taking this latest book as gospel. At the same time, even if these results exaggerate, the picture is worrying. It may not be so much that we lack a common morality but that under certain circumstances too many of us are prepared to chuck our morality overboard.

That was a point recently made by Portland Police Chief Tom Potter when he talked about people who disobeyed laws because the laws were inconvenient to them. The chief has been pilloried for his efforts to end jaywalking. But, as he said on the KATU-TV *Town Hall* program entitled "Cheaters," what he was trying to do was to underline individual responsibility in our society. An individual jaywalk might be regarded by some as innocuous but each act has to be multiplied by a hundred thousand acts. And people die as a result. "If a few people disobey the law," he said, "the police can contain the situation. But when everybody breaks the law we can't." "Who is responsible for fixing the problems?" he asked. "Who is responsible for your children, for your neighborhood, your community? We're saying you are, the individual citizen. You have to start in your own backyard."

The chief's words remind me of the Michael Jackson song, "I'm starting with the man in the mirror. I'm asking him to make a change. If you want to see the world a different place. Take a look at yourself and make a change."

Or as that old religious song put it, "The devil is a rascal kick him out." Though, sensitive to some of today's modern theology, I might have to correct that to "kick her out."

30 APRIL 1991

May Americans listen

A MOSCOW JOURNALIST gets up and calls for Russian repentance. "We Soviets are guilty before so many peoples," he says. A grandson of Stalin's foreign minister calls for "breaking the circle of hatred." A Hungarian under-secretary of state talks of the need for co-operation with Austria and Czechoslovakia in tackling the ecological disaster created by damming the

Danube. The doyen of the Polish senate foresees the ending of the "mad" contrasts between the two halves of Europe. "We have crossed the threshold to a new era," he says.

All these speakers were addressing the Moral Re-Armament conference in Caux, Switzerland which drew several thousand people from all over the world. Its theme, "Freeing the forces of change."

Writing from Caux, syndicated columnist Georgie Anne Geyer pointed out that most people, if asked about Moral Re-Armament, would "remember its excellent work to heal the devastation of postwar Europe when men hungry for meaning, such as Konrad Adenauer and Robert Schuman, were inspired by it."

The Caux conference began to see that work of healing extended to the spiritual devastation in Eastern Europe. Though it was clear, as those from East and West met, that the healing process was not a one-way street. A senior French member of parliament pointed out, "Democracy in many of our West European countries looks tired. We need a replenishment of soul that the people of the East will give us filtered through the sufferings of half a century of struggle."

Many years ago Frank Buchman, the initiator of Moral Re-Armament, had said to his younger colleagues, "One day some of you will be working in Moscow." At the time it seemed most unlikely. Now it is happening. One of the most stirring experiences for me at the conference was to meet a senior editor from the Soviet news agency Novosti, now the government's information arm, whom I had welcomed to Caux more than 20 years earlier. After he left Caux on that occasion he wrote a strong attack on its work in *Izvestia*. Now he was apologizing for what he had written and saying that in welcoming him back we had turned the other cheek. It will be interesting to see what he writes this time.

Another moving encounter this summer was when a group

of twenty young Romanians met with King Michael, who had been ousted by the Communists at the point of a gun. They had been brought up on a completely fictional account of his past, even to the point of being told that he could not speak Romanian. They spent hours together, conversing in Romanian about the modern history of their country. One of the Romanian students had brought with him drawings to sell to raise money towards the cost of their stay in Caux. He presented one to the king. It was of the king's summer palace where he grew up as a boy. A friend of the king commented, "He looks ten years younger."

The languages of Eastern Europe pouring out of the translators' booths, Russian productions mounted in the Caux theater, seminars on the Baltic republics, a Bulgarian cutting out the Communist emblem in a flag, all emphasized the momentous changes going on in that part of the world.

There were many telling glimpses and encounters from other parts of the world:

The Fijian chief who apologized to the Indian community for leading a violent movement to oust them from his island country.

The prime minister of the national government of Cambodia who had come to regenerate his spiritual batteries.

The pains of an African National Congress man from South Africa who had been held for 21 years on Robben Island, and of a Cambodian who was a survivor of "the killing fields."

A Pole who came to Caux last year as a Solidarity militant with prison and persecution behind him and returned this year as mayor of Lodz.

A young Brazilian who was a drug pusher and is now a responsible leader of a housing community in Rio.

A Cypriot couple, who had been forced to flee from their home with nothing but the front door key, speaking on "finding freedom from blame."

Twelve black teenagers from Atlanta who have contributed to the decline in violence in the public schools of their city.

A Berlin couple who had found healing and an answer to bitterness over sexual abuse in their family.

At one session, held as dusk fell, audience members were invited to light candles and pray for different parts of the world—Northern Ireland, Lebanon, China, Soweto, Cambodia, Burma, the children of the world. So many concerns. Said a young American girl as she lit a candle: "May we Americans learn to listen to all these voices."

6 SEPTEMBER 1990

8   On library shelves

In Portland's Multnomah County Library there's a room
to the left as you come in that houses paperbacks and new
fiction and art for hire and teenage magazines and mystery
novels and large print books and a few tables and chairs.
Sitting there are all sorts of people, some simply passing the
time away, some perhaps sheltering from the rain, some
reading, some studying. Is there a literary giant among them?

Sixty years ago a young man used to frequent that library.
He was a worker in a veneer plant, it was the time of the
depression, and often there was not enough work to warrant
a full shift. So nearly every day for months he would head for
the library where he read the books of Conrad, Tagore, and
Wells, the plays of O'Neill, Racine, and Shaw, the philosophy
of Santayana, Nietzsche, and Schopenhauer.

The young man who spent those hours in the Library went
on to produce eighty-six novels, sixteen short-story collec-
tions, and three works of non-fiction. He is the only novelist
to receive both the Congressional Gold Medal and the Presidential Medal of Freedom. More than 200 million copies of
his books are in print.

Louis L'Amour died in 1988. We know what he owed to

the Multnomah County Library through his fascinating book *Education of a Wandering Man*. "Upon the shelves of our libraries," L'Amour writes, "the world's greatest teachers await our questions. Our libraries are not cloisters for an elite. They are for the people, and if they are not used, the fault belongs to those who do not take advantage of their wealth. If one does not move on from what merely amuses to what interests, the fault lies in the reader, for everything is there."

Grandfather Dictionary

LAST WEEK I happened to step on the connection box for my computer just as my daughter, Juliet, was finishing a paper. The computer switched off and she lost an hour's work. I won't hear the end of that for a long time. Such are the perils of this modern age.

I marvel at how far we've come. Only 5 years ago I was still typing articles, commentaries and letters on a little portable typewriter I used for 30 years. Then I was given an electric typewriter, which amazed me, and in short order that was followed by a computer that I don't even begin to understand.

Except for the occasional frustrating disappearance of a text like my daughter's paper, the possibilities that a word processor opens up are now taken for granted. I can only marvel at the productivity of earlier generations working with a quill pen and often by candlelight. The nearest I come to that was trying to work by lantern light in a Nigerian village. In the same way it is a source of the greatest admiration how dissident voices in the Soviet Union have been able laboriously to produce samizdat without access to photocopiers.

Perhaps the most remarkable example of the advantage of the modern word processor over the different methods of our predecessors is the second, when compared with the first, edition of *The Oxford English Dictionary*. The second edition has twenty volumes, 21,728 pages, 616,500 entries, uses 60 million words and 2.5 million quotations. It was completed in only seven years, as projected, thanks to computerization, and is now in a data base. To assemble the 350 million printed characters took 120 person years of keyboarding and 60 person years of proofreading and was a cooperative venture between Britain, Canada, and the United States, where it was also printed and bound.

The first edition was begun in 1879 with the expectation it would take 10 years and be 6400 pages. It actually took 54 years and turned out to be 15,500 pages. It was done entirely by hand. As there were no photocopiers in those days, even early editions of books from previous centuries were torn apart to be filed with the reference slips under the different letters of the alphabet. Copies exist of the handwritten texts prepared for the printers by editor James Murray.

This second edition successfully integrates the thirteen volumes of the first edition, and supplementary volumes, incorporating some 5000 new words. Thanks to Murray's logical system, the dictionary was easily computerized. I feel a personal link with the dictionary for James Murray was a teacher at Mill Hill School in London, which I attended, and did much of his early work on it there. I used to visit regularly the Murray Scriptorium to read the newspapers, where we were surveyed by an imposing photograph of the long-bearded philological giant. It would be nice to think it was the same scriptorium in which he worked but this was the replacement of the original, which burned down in 1902.

Grandfather Dictionary, as he was known by his family, only lived to see it half completed, though he laid the plan for the whole. In a sermon he once said, "Every man is given a life work to accomplish." He saw the work on the dictionary not only as his life's work but also as God's will for him. Good work once done and in print, he said, then becomes an eternal inheritance which will remain of value to generations to come. And so it has proved. For *The Oxford English Dictionary* is not just a book of words, but as John Agresto, president of the Madison Center in Washington, D.C., points out, "It comes close to being the collected library and intellectual heritage of the whole English-speaking world."

9 MAY 1989

The heart of Islam

The Oregonian recently carried an op-ed article by Middle East expert Charis Waddy, in which she argued that the building of friendship with the people of the Middle East was not only vital but was one of "the powerful, unseen growth patterns of our times."

I showed her words to a friend who, after reading the first few paragraphs in which it was stated that forty-eight countries in the world have a Muslim majority, said, "Oh, isn't that terrible." Her remark underlined how much work has to be done to educate the public about the Muslim world.

Australian-born Charis Waddy, a devout Christian and author of several books on the Middle East, knows her subject well. She was the first woman to study Arabic and Hebrew at Oxford University. Her doctorate at London University was on the Arab side of the Crusades. She was one of two women delegates at Muslim congresses in Pakistan and Turkey, and has lectured in Jerusalem and Cairo.

Last year she was decorated by the government of Pakistan. In fact, the former Pakistani prime minister, Benazir Bhutto, attended the British launching of the new English edition of her book *The Muslim Mind*, published in the United States by New Amsterdam Books.

Some years ago Professor Noury Al-Khaledy, distinguished former head of Middle East studies at Portland State University, conducted a study of an earlier edition of *The Muslim Mind* when the author visited Oregon. He was impressed with Dr. Waddy's work, he said, because her descriptions of Islam were not documented from books but extracted from people, and not only from leading people who were sometimes unrepresentative but from all levels of society. She had not restricted herself to Egypt or Arabia, or the Persians and the Turks and generalized from there but, he said, had "gone as far as Malaysia." The book was up to date and related to everyday life.

Dr. Al Khaledy said that after working in the field for 25 years he should now be bored by books on such a subject, but he couldn't wait to finish it. He had had unhappy experiences with books that purported to get into the Muslim mind. "But it amazed me. I have never seen so far anybody who has written about Islam truthfully with an understanding like this author." He described her as not only an historian but a woman with a mission. "She's interested in human beings and the world. What she is doing and can be done is working towards understanding and world community. I admire it. It's what we need in this world."

Dr. Waddy started compiling *The Muslim Mind* in the wake of the Arab-Israeli 6-day war. She felt the need for a book that would give Muslims the chance of expressing for the West what they really believe and think. One of those who most encouraged her was a former Iraqi prime minister, who gave her the Arab proverb, "What comes from the mouth reaches only to the ear. What comes from the heart reaches the heart."

At the London book launching she pointed out that Iraq (Mesopotamia) had known its tyrants in the past, like Nebuchadnezzar. But it had also given to the world Abraham, a towering figure in the history of mankind. "Judaism, Christianity, and Islam," she said, "all stemmed from the faith of that friend of God and father of believers. The dawn of a new cooperation between the servants of the one God," she believes, "may be an unexpected and hopeful factor in the coming years."

This new edition of *The Muslim Mind* contains all the features on the world of Islam that won praise for the last edition, and includes new material based on new conversations with Muslims in many lands. Dr. Waddy writes in the book, "Old clichés which have been locks on the doors of understanding can be disregarded. Ears can be opened to hear the call to prayer and hearts to appreciate the wisdom and grace of a lifestyle other than our own."

The Muslim Mind is a significant contribution to that end.

7 MARCH 1991

Have book, will travel

I WAS INVITED out to dinner once in India. I arrived at 6 o'clock as arranged. But come 9 o'clock and then 9:30 with no sign of dinner, I thought I must have made a mistake and was just preparing to say goodbye when a sumptuous feast arrived. In England when you are invited for dinner, you eat first and talk afterwards. In India you talk first and eat afterwards. This custom has advantages, I must admit, as it helps avoid those times, rare, of course, when as hosts you would like to go to bed but your guests just keep on talking. When you've finished the meal in India you are expected to leave.

I went to a meeting in New Zealand to plan a big theater evening. A thousand guests were expected for a first night. Someone suggested serving supper to the whole audience. The idea was accepted without demur. Knowing the financial limitations of the organizers and mulling over the logistic problems of such a bold gesture, I marveled at the generosity of the hosts. It was only afterwards I discovered that supper in New Zealand and in Australia does not mean an evening meal but simply a cold drink.

There's so much to learn about the ways and customs of other countries. I have often wished there were a comprehensive book to help you get things right in somebody else's country. And now one has been published. It's entitled *Do's and Taboos Around the World* and is edited by Roger E. Axtell and compiled by the Parker Pen Company, which has offices in 154 countries.

The book deals with protocol, customs and etiquette, and subjects like gift giving and receiving. It has a whole section on hand gestures and body language, which underlines the fact that an innocent gesture acceptable in one culture could be regarded as obscene in another. I came to the conclusion after looking at its illustrated international dictionary of gestures that I would be safest to cut all hand gestures to a minimum.

There is also a section on American jargon and baffling idioms. This could well be read with benefit by non-overseas travelers. As one paragraph warns, "Keep in mind that your English-as-a-second-language business counterpart may take your words quite literally. One midwestern executive sent a cable to his Peruvian manager saying, 'Send me factory and office headcount broken down by sex.' The reply came, '249 in factory, 30 in office, 3 on sick leave, none broken down by sex —our problem is with alcohol.'"

I read the section on Britain with interest. It is almost accurate. And, having been away 10 years, I was pleased to learn that it is still not proper at a formal dinner to smoke until after the toast to the Queen.

The comparison of cultures contains occasional advice that might well be adopted here. The book speaks of the gap between Japanese who regard silence as an important aspect of clear communications and the Americans who abhor it.

Among the Japanese it is common, even expected, to have periods of silence in which the Japanese executive contemplates what has been said. The Japanese cannot understand why an American dislikes those quiet moments. As one Japanese executive asked, "Do American businesspeople think and talk at the same time?"

I have one reservation about *Do's and Taboos Around the World*. It lists so many things that you might do wrong or say wrongly that you could be tempted to stay home instead. But, having spent time in thirty or so countries, I can assure you that if you are willing to restrain an inherent boisterousness and treat other people with the graciousness with which you would like to be treated you'll get on fine, even if you don't go by the book.

27 JUNE 1989

No scapegoats

WHEN LORD CARRINGTON resigned as British defence secretary at the time of the Argentine invasion of the Falkland Islands, many well-meaning people tried to talk him out of it. But he felt it was the right thing to do. Not out of a sense of blame but because the country felt angry and humiliated and if he had stayed it would have made it harder for the government. As he wrote, "My departure would put a stop to the search for scapegoats. It would serve the cause of unity and help turn the eyes of all from the past to the immediate future." His action reflects his high standards of public service, which some might regard as old-fashioned. It also opened the way for him to become secretary-general of NATO for 4 years. Lord Carrington served in every conservative government from Churchill's of 1951 to Mrs. Thatcher's of 1979. And a member of the House of Lords I talked with regrets that he is not a candidate to succeed the Iron Lady.

I have just been reading his memoirs, *Reflect On Things Past*, and its pages reflect the basic decency of the man. There are many short sketches of others in public life and it is noticeable that those of whom he thinks highly are identified and many of those that he feels behaved badly remain nameless. There is enough humor in the book for former Labor Foreign Secretary David Owen to comment, "Some jokes leave me still chuckling" and enough substance on issues as varied as nuclear deterrence and the independence of Zimbabwe for the *Times Literary Supplement* reviewer to call *Reflect on Things Past* "a serious and thoughtful retrospect of foreign policy over thirty years."

We are introduced to an entertaining account of earlier lords Carrington. These include his great uncle, who was so incensed by a scurrilous attack on his father by a journalist that he purchased a rhinoceros-hide whip, beat the unfortunate man on the steps of the Conservative Club, and then went to nearby Pratt's Club where he asked friends to testify to the fact that he was neither excited nor drunk. This Lord Carrington was put on probation, but the journalist, charged with perjury, fled the country. The present Lord Carrington says he never belonged to the Conservative Club but might have had difficulty joining because those at this respectable institution have long memories!

Lord Carrington's memoirs span his life at Eton College; his time in the Grenadier Guards, including service in Europe in World War II; his experiences in government and opposition, in agriculture and defence; and his stint as governor general of Australia. Incidentally, he tells a delightful cricket story from his stay in Australia. After an international match one evening in Adelaide he found himself with Australia's greatest cricketer Donald Bradman, and cricket commentator Brian Johnston. Brian criticized Australian umpiring and a particularly controversial decision that afternoon. "I can't understand how he can have given him out," said Brian. "He doesn't know the rules of the game. He can't have played cricket in his life."

Bradman got angry. "Hasn't played cricket," he roared. "He played for Australia. In fact, he'd be playing still, if his eyesight hadn't failed."

He has other delightful vignettes. For instance, Field Marshal Viscount Montgomery greeting him with the words, "How do you do, have you met me before?" Lord Carrington's comment: "I had never heard it put quite like that." And Prime Minister Macmillan, chided by a British ambassador for a rather disagreeable remark he had made about Senator Muskie. The ambassador said, "How would you like it if you were at a meeting in your constituency and someone from the back of the hall yelled out 'Lady Dorothy Macmillan is an old drunk.' How would you react?" Macmillan replied, "Ah, I would shout back, 'You should have seen her mother.'"

Summing up his views, Lord Carrington says that he is a vigorous opponent of those who cherish a nostalgic and absurdly grandiose image of Britain's modern destiny, an opponent of those who resent or reject Britain's place as a European nation, and also an opponent of the unfeeling, the inwardly callous (however smooth-spoken), the hard-hearted people in politics, the cynics.

He has always believed in the necessity to see the points of view of others and to try to see how others look at Britain. For arrogance and insensitivity, he believes, come too easily to a people that hold an inflated view of their own rights and importance.

"I have been in politics," he concludes, "because I have enjoyed it, have loved my country, and wanted to contribute to governing it. The simple ideas I have spent much of the time trying to promote are those of the fortunate sharing responsibility for those less so; and of our nation, vigorous to defend itself if attacked, seeking harmony and genuine understanding with others in a world where Britain, good-natured, good-tempered and good-mannered Britain, has a limited but still significant and honorable role to play."

Reflect On Things Past is not, then, the retailing of scandal, or the getting back at opponents, or the source book for sensational headlines. Rather, it is a book that makes you wish that more people in public life had the motivation of the sixth Lord Carrington.

22 FEBRUARY 1990

Tutu's master

WHAT SHOULD we make of the Right Reverend Desmond Tutu, first black Anglican archbishop of Cape Town?

To many people he is a hero, if not a saint. One Oregon church has even considered whether to put him in a stained glass window. He was awarded, as most of you know, the Nobel Peace Prize for 1984. I have in my own mind the image of him, a small figure, courageously wading into a volatile crowd to try to save the life of a black man who was accused of being an informer and telling the crowd that he would leave South Africa if his people did not desist from murder.

The late Percy Quboza, a distinguished black editor who was present at that occasion, told a Harvard audience that he and his friends were scared stiff for Tutu. Armed police were all round. If he had been shot no one would have believed it wasn't by a white man. "We tried to get Tutu out," he said, "but we couldn't because Tutu obeys his master."

On the other hand to many people Tutu is a devil. South African diplomatic or consular officials who come to town often make some denigrating remark about him. The last two items I read about him in our newspapers concerned his June 1988 visit to the Soviet Union to join ecumenical celebrations of the thousandth anniversary of the Russian Orthodox Church. He thanked the Soviets, one report said, "for their prayers and for their support, moral and humanitarian," in the fight against apartheid.

I have before me as I write a photo of the controversial archbishop giving what the caption says is the Marxist power salute at the first gathering of the National Forum for Black Consciousness in June 1983. He is quoted as saying, "There comes a time when it is justifiable to overthrow an unjust system by violence." And judicial enquiry into the finances of the South African Council of Churches while he was its head revealed considerable misuse of funds.

So I was delighted to pick up a newly published, authoritative and authorized biography of the South African priest. It is entitled *Tutu—Voice of the Voiceless* and is written by Shirley du Boulay, a former BBC producer and the author of an earlier, critically acclaimed biography of Dame Cicely Saunders, founder of the modern hospice movement.

Du Boulay goes carefully into all sides of Tutu's life, sweeping nothing under the rug, confronting the uncomfortable as well as recounting the inspirational. Her book gives the reader a good idea of the difficulties encountered growing up black in South Africa and the reader recognizes Tutu's remarkable achievement in just getting where he is. Stanley Uys, reviewing the book on the BBC World Service, said that "if fault has to be found it is a shade too reverential." I wouldn't put it quite that way. I think I would rather say that she writes with her heart on her sleeve and sometimes feels the need to underscore unfairness and belabor those who practice it rather than letting the reader draw the same conclusion from hearing the facts. But that is hardly a weakness. It would be an unfeeling person who could study the evidence and not deal sympathetically with the archbishop.

I have come to the conclusion after reading the book that our reactions to Tutu may say more about us and our philosophy and values than they do about him. One of the problems faced by public figures, perhaps today more than ever, is the perfection expected by the public. And whether someone strives to be a leader or is thrust by events, as Tutu has been, into a leadership position, he or she will have weaknesses. I form the impression that Tutu can be short-tempered, that he may be a little naive politically, that he may not be up to being cast as the savior of his country. I do not fully subscribe to his view that God takes sides. But I must say that I prefer his views to some of the views of his most outspoken critics. And he needs to be listened to.

Tutu—Voice of the Voiceless gives a real feel for the man and his concerns, the influences on his life, some of which are surprising, and his hopes for his country. It certainly ought to be read by all who want to understand South Africa better. I hope that it will be widely read by whites in South Africa, most of whom still have little idea what it means to be an intelligent, highly educated, deeply Christian man, let alone an archbishop and a Nobel laureate, who cannot even vote in his own country.

By chance, I have been reading at the same time another book, *South Africa: Revolution or Reconciliation*, by Walter H. Kansteiner. This is a valuable, dispassionate look at the South African scene in an attempt to find a non-violent way forward. If it has a weakness it is that it lacks the flesh-and-blood quality of the Tutu book and in its cerebral approach tries to make too tidy a package of people and events that defy precise ideological labeling. I would like my liberal friends to read it as much as I would like my conservative friends to know Tutu.

25 AUGUST 1988

A wondering minstrel he

I HAVE JUST read a book of questions. But, unlike many books of questions, you can't look up the answers in the back. You have to think them out for yourself. It has an apt title, *I Was Just Wondering*.

The book contains forty-five of the best columns that Philip Yancey has written for *Christianity Today* and is published by Eerdmans. A prolific and provocative author, Yancey has had more than 400 articles in sixty publications and his nine books include *Where is God When It Hurts?* and his recent best seller *Disappointment with God*, named in April 1990 as Book of the Year by the readers of *Christianity Today* and called by its critics the best book on Christian living and spirituality.

Yancey's inquiring mind attracts a large volume of letters from readers of *Christianity Today* and he says that it was a column consisting entirely of questions that drew the largest response. His subjects range from adultery to Alcoholics Anonymous, from Habitat for Humanity to hospitals in India, from arranged marriages to a post mortem of PTL. And I suppose the best way to review his book is to pass on some of his questions and his wondering about them. For, as *Moody Monthly* writes, "Yancey speaks with a clear and intelligent voice and presumes the reader can think for himself."

"Why is it," Yancey asks, "that the most beautiful animals on earth are hidden away from all humans except those wearing elaborate scuba equipment? Who are they beautiful for? Why did Solomon, who showed such wisdom in writing proverbs, spend the last years of his life breaking all those proverbs? Does God love Americans more than Iranians?"

Yancey makes penetrating comments on the issues in the news, secular and religious. On arms for hostages he asks, "How many foreigners' deaths are worth six American lives?" On AIDS he says, "I have yet to find any support in the Bible for smugness." On PTL, "I doubt very seriously that the watching world had any longings for God awakened, or caught a glimpse of the difference God can make in a transformed people. Tragically, the evangelicals who dominated the news in 1987 and 1988 came across looking just like everybody else, only more so."

Having had the chance to interview diverse people, he would divide them into two types: stars and servants. He says that the famous people and idols we fawn over are in his experience as miserable a group of people as he has ever met, nearly all hopelessly dependent on psychotherapy. He maintains that "in a heavy irony these larger-than-life heroes seem tormented by incurable self-doubt." But, he says, he encounters the same problem with the Christian stars.

Meeting many excuses from friends for their behavior in their mid-life crisis, he says he feels like handing each a copy of *Anna Karenina*, which he insists says everything worth saying about their supposed unique experiences of passion, love, boredom, selfishness, and lust. "I have more appreciation," he writes, "for why the Bible avoids fuzzy psychologisms and says simply to the stealer 'Steal no more' and to the tempted 'Flee temptation.'" In his view the Bible challenges us to look upward, not inward, for counsel at moments of crisis. He quotes Jeremiah, "The heart is deceitful above all things and beyond cure. Who can understand it?" Not very sophisticated-sounding advice, to be sure, he admits, "but then some of our modern advice gets so sophisticated," he says, "that it soars beyond the realm of rational coherence."

In one essay he asks, "Wouldn't a phrase like repentant majority or forgiven majority serve as a more orthodox way of defining Christians than moral majority?" In another he warns about the temptations of power in the Christian community. "Jesus did not say, 'All men will know you are my disciples ... if you just pass laws, quash immorality, and restore decency to family and government' but rather 'if you love one another.'"

The most moving piece in the book, which I will not attempt to reproduce in brief, deals with Nazi evil and the death camps and forgiveness and the beast that is in all of us. He quotes one man who asks, "I sometimes wonder what might have happened if a skilled, sensitive person had befriended the young, impressionable Adolf Hitler as he wandered the streets of Vienna in his confused state."

On one page Yancey asks, "Why is sex pleasurable, why is eating fun, why are there colors?" and comments, "I'm still waiting for a good explanation that does not include the word 'God.'"

It is not difficult to see why *Library Journal* in an enthusiastic recommendation of *I Was Just Wondering* can write, "When Yancey couples his vibrant curiosity with his felicitous style and then begins reflecting on everything under the sun, the result is a collection of stimulating observations bound to nudge and encourage a reader's own reflective powers."

3 MAY 1990

Bad news is news

IN SOME WAYS journalism is the enemy of normality. What is normal is assumed, not reported. Everything, to a journalist, has to be growing or collapsing. "America is in decline." "America is now the one superpower." "Support for policies is increasing." "Support is decreasing." "Racial violence is mounting." "Hate crimes are declining." Indeed, political scientist Leo Rosten defines news as "the departure from the normal." Or, as Henry Luce told President Johnson, "Good news isn't news. Bad news is news."

So it is not surprising that a new book of anecdotes of American journalism should include stories of men and women whose activities do not make them good role models for today.

Fortunately, just as the average reader knows not to take too seriously everything in the papers, so the readers of *If No News, Send Rumors* will relish this book but also realize that not all its cast of characters are typical of the normal, hard-working, ethical journalist.

The book reflects changing attitudes. When a prototype television was demonstrated at the 1939 World's Fair, the *New York Times* reviewer wrote, "The problem with television is that the people must sit and keep their eyes glued on a screen; the average American family hasn't time for it."

The New York City Police Department allowed Walter Winchell to have a siren on his car and he often blasted it as he drove round New York City, always turning it off as he approached his own house because, he explained, he didn't want to wake his children.

Twenty years ago women writers at the *Washington Post*, protesting sexism at the paper, distributed this piece:

> Ben Bradlee, slim, attractive, but complex executive editor of the *Washington Post* is 49 years old today, but he doesn't look it. How does he manage to combine a successful career with the happy home life he has created in his gracious Georgetown home?
>
> In an interview today, pert, vivacious Mr. Bradlee revealed his secret. He relaxes after a day of whirlwind activity of the newspaper world by whomping up a batch of his favorite pecan-sauerbraten cookies for his thriving family.
>
> What does Mrs. Bradlee think of her debonair husband's flair for journalism? 'I think it's great,' she said. 'Every wife should let her husband work. It makes him so well-rounded. Now he has something to talk about at the dinner table.'
>
> She appreciates the extra effort he takes to maintain his youthful looks and figure despite his busy, busy day. Mr. Bradlee loves his work, but he is aware of the dangers involved. So far he does not feel in competition with his wife.
>
> 'When that day comes,' he said with a shudder, 'I'll know it's time to quit.'
>
> Mr. Bradlee's quick and easy recipe for pecan-sauerbraten cookies appears in tomorrow's bulletin.

Papers, of course, are always on the lookout for local angles. A San Fernando Valley radio station began one newscast,

"Two high-speed trains collided today between Tokyo and Osaka, Japan. There were one hundred twenty-three people killed and several hundred have been injured. But there were no Valley residents on board."

I liked the remark of a student after hearing Bill Moyers deliver a commencement address: "Mr. Moyers, you've been in both journalism and government. That makes everything you say doubly hard to believe."

I also enjoyed the selection of dream leads to stories, which included this one from Jack Anderson's assistant, Les Whitten: "Jesus Christ, whose second coming has been promised for almost two thousand years, landed at Washington National Airport secretly today and confided his plans exclusively to this reporter."

It is interesting to reflect, with the demise of communism, that in 1851 Karl Marx was invited by the *New York Tribune* to become its London correspondent. Short of money he gratefully accepted. In 1862, however, the paper's editor told him his services were no longer needed; the paper was devoting less space to foreign coverage. He didn't mention that he had discovered that Marx was billing the paper for articles he hadn't yet written. Marx then resumed his political writing. President Kennedy was to remark a century later, "If only Marx had remained a foreign correspondent history might have been different."

In short, *If No News, Send Rumors* is a most enjoyable book, one you can dip into at will. I don't think author Stephen Bates pretends to take a serious look at the profession. But it's a darn good read. And I imagine that many of the anecdotes will find their way into speeches in the year ahead.

The book's title dates from the Civil War when the *Chicago Times* editor Wilbur F. Storey instructed a correspondent, "Telegraph fully all news you can get and when there is no news send rumors."

7 FEBRUARY 1991

Frank Buchman

NATIVE AMERICANS made him a blood brother with the name Great Light Out Of Darkness. The National Association of Colored Women's Clubs awarded him a permanent trophy as "the greatest humanitarian of them all." Seven countries decorated him for his work of reconciliation. Brother Roger, of Taizé, spoke of him as a saint. To me, however, he was just Frank.

I refer to Frank Buchman, the initiator of Moral Re-Armament and the subject of a major biography, *On the Tail of a Comet*. I first met him when I was 15, and later worked with him for 10 years in the United States, Europe, and Asia. So I am particularly pleased that his stature can now be recognized in his own country. For he is, as the book's subtitle says, "A small town American who awakened the conscience of the world."

For anyone interested in the history of this century, in the clash of ideologies, in the role of faith in the public arena, in how to live life to the fullest, or just in a superbly written biography, I recommend *On the Tail of a Comet*.

I am sorry that I never experienced Buchman when he had full vigor. I only knew him after a paralyzing stroke that made him dependent on others to get around. But even then he was a dynamo as he tried to follow his own advice of thinking and living for continents. Early on, he outlined his aim as "a program of life issuing in personal, social, racial, national, and supernational change."

Buchman was not good-looking or charismatic, he was no orator, he never wrote books. Yet he gathered around him a team of highly talented men and women, was constantly sought out for advice by those in positions of leadership, and inspired the writing of hundreds of books. Author Garth Lean, asked in an interview for the BBC why people were attracted to him, said, "You felt that he was in touch with God." Buchman himself said, "I always liked people." Indeed, his encounters with, and sometimes profound effect on, some key twentieth-century personalities make gripping reading.

Many initiatives in the modern world flowed from his touch with people, not the least Alcoholics Anonymous (whose twelve steps are based on his approach), which has been a godsend to millions. Lloyd Douglas, author of *The Robe*, said Buchman had "a Napoleonic gift of making people do hard things."

Although Buchman's work drew headlines and involved at times mass meetings, he thought always in terms of individuals. He was skeptical, as he put it, of "applying eye medicine from a second-story window," or of "chasing rabbits with a brass band." He believed first and foremost in changing people, starting with the person in front of him. That is clear from the book.

Buchman was always alert to what God might be saying to other people, expecting them to come up with inspiration. He got his concept of absolute honesty, purity, unselfishness, and love from a book on the life of Jesus. He drew the emphasis on listening for God's direction from a Christian teacher. He even derived the name Moral Re-Armament from a Swedish writer.

Today it is normal to think in terms of faith being something that has outreach into all areas of life, of different faiths working together, of the importance of meditation, or silence, or listening, but these were all things he fought for when it was less fashionable. Perhaps his insistence on absolute moral standards is more relevant today than ever.

In an age before TV he was a master at telling stories of change that gripped the imagination and challenged the will. It would be hard to imagine him, however, as a TV preacher. For one thing he never appealed publicly for money and was scrupulously correct in accounting for money given.

Buchman's purpose, Lean writes, was entirely positive: "He never organized a protest against anything, still less denounced anyone in public. His response to every difficulty was faith that God could change people, and the more serious he perceived the state of the world to be, the more intensely he concentrated on individuals."

Lean sees Buchman's greatest achievement as the creation of a world-wide network of people committed to carry on the same work, in the words of the former archbishop of York, Lord Blanch, ready to go anywhere and do anything if they are called by God to do it.

From a profound experience of change and the answer to bitterness in his own life, he went on to develop an approach that helped millions find that same liberation. From a conventional Christian upbringing, he went beyond the confines of conventional religion in a way that won the confidence of leaders of other faiths as well. As tennis player Arthur Ashe says of *On the Tail of a Comet*, "It just goes to show what one man can do when absolutely dedicated to morally just ends."

21 JULY 1985

They would fight the waves

THE FIGHTING SPIRIT of the Irish is legendary. "Is this a private fight," an Irishman is supposed to have once asked, "or may everyone join in?" That apocryphal quip came to mind after I had finished reading a magnificent new book, *A History of the Irish Soldier*.

For those of us who are English of a certain generation the names Alanbrooke, Alexander, Auckinleck, Dill, and Montgomery conjure up a picture of excellence in military leadership in World War II, to which we all owe a great deal. Not everyone knows, however, that these men are all Irish field marshals. Indeed, Montgomery is regarded as the best British field commander since the Duke of Wellington, also Irish.

Some half a million Irish are reckoned to have served with the British Army in World War I, with 50,000 dying on the battlefields. All of them were volunteers, as were the 165,000 from the Irish Republic who fought for Britain in World War II. *A History of the Irish Soldier* is dedicated to them and "to all Irish soldiers throughout the ages who fought the good fight for the justice of their particular cause."

Looking at my Irish family tree I have always been struck by the numbers who were in the army—I count a dozen British and Irish regiments listed. So I found this new book fascinating. The author, Brigadier A.E.C. Bredin, himself an Irish soldier of distinction, has assembled in one 550-page volume probably the first comprehensive attempt to tell the remarkable story of the Irish soldier down the ages and across the continents.

Published by Century Books of Belfast, *A History of the Irish Soldier* contains hundreds of maps, illustrations, and photographs, and has the quality of a coffee table book. As General Sir John Hackett, another Irishman, says in his foreword, "These were perhaps the best fighting men the world has ever seen." Spurred on, he says, by "poverty, politics, and pugnacity," they fought everywhere with high distinction and became the first embodiment of Irish nationhood.

From ancient Grecian times, where we find Aristotle writing of Keltoi living by the Caspian who were "so fierce and warlike that when they had no one to fight they would dash into the sea to fight the waves," to the modern blue-bereted United Nations peace-keeping forces, wherever there have been battles, there have been Irishmen. So it is a wide canvas on which Brigadier Bredin has to paint.

The Irish, because of their history, are often to be found fighting on both sides. Their names rather than their uniforms betray their origins: Russian Field Marshal Peter De Lacy, Marshal of France Patrice Maurice McMahon, Prussian Field Marshal William O'Kelly, Spanish Captain-General Alexander O'Reilly, Director Supremo Bernard O'Higgins, to whom

Chile owes its independence. They are among the characters who enliven the pages.

American readers will be interested in the Irish participation on both sides in the Revolutionary War and the Civil War. Watching one Irish brigade attack as part of the Union army, a reporter from *The Times* of London wrote, "Never at Fontenoy, Albuera, or Waterloo was more courage displayed by the sons of Erin." When Chief Sitting Bull died, a medal was found on his body that had been taken from an Irish soldier who had been killed in Custer's last stand.

This is not a book for everyone; it is too detailed. But it is a must for military buffs and for those who take pride in the feats of the Irish. Not every judgment will be accepted by every reader. Brigadier Bredin is a British military man and does not pretend otherwise. *A History of the Irish Soldier* is obviously a labor of love and also a work of scholarship even though the author calls himself "a simple Irish soldier."

4 AUGUST 1988

A God who speaks

FORTY YEARS AGO I set my feet on the road of a big adventure. It has taken me around the world and to experiences that range from working backstage on Broadway to acting before thousands in Africa, from reporting Commonwealth Heads of Government meetings to documenting secretly the abuse of human rights in an Asian country. It has involved me in a wonderful network of friendships with people whose lives are committed to building a different kind of world. It has naturally encompassed great hopes, some great disappointments, and great satisfaction. And all this has been based on a very simple premise: that God can guide people who are willing to turn their lives over to him.

Early on I was introduced to the idea that when people listen

God speaks, when they obey God acts. I was taught to rise early to take time to listen, a discipline I first began as an irksome experiment but which has since become a daily necessity. It is something my wife and I do every morning, and whenever during the day we feel the need for it. I have "listened to God" with Indian villagers and Nigerian cabinet ministers, with people in public life and ordinary citizens, and in all sorts of circumstances—even in one case sitting in the back of the Queen of England's Rolls Royce! I have seen the difference this discipline can make in my own life and in the life of others.

Over the years I have also seen the havoc that misuse of the idea of God's guidance can cause in people's lives and been saddened by the way this has inoculated people against this life-enhancing experience.

Sorting out what is and what is not God's will is far from easy. Though it is less complicated once you have decided you want it. I was taught certain safeguards and tests. For, after all, it is very easy to kid yourself that what you want is God's will or, in certain traditions, what you want can't be God's will. One test was to measure the thoughts I had in times of quiet against the teachings of my faith and against absolute moral standards of honesty, purity, unselfishness, and love.

So I was particularly pleased to receive recently a new book by a distinguished theologian, Klaus Bockmuehl, which introduces us biblically to the precedent and practice of "listening." Klaus, who was professor of theology at Regent College, Vancouver, B.C., and whom I knew most of the 40 years I have followed this way of life, had the scholarship as well as the practical application to deal authoritatively with this subject. He labored to finish this book before he died of cancer. It is aptly entitled *Listening to the God Who Speaks*, and is a worthy successor to his book *Living by the Gospel*. It is published by Helmers and Howard.

In a foreword Dr. James Houston, the eminent theologian, describes *Listening to the God Who Speaks* as "very much a last will and testament to the church from one of its most faithful and obedient sons." He writes, "Here is a testimony of a life given to God, to be his listener. It is my prayer that this book will become a classic of devotion for all those who likewise have ears to hear."

In his book Klaus points out that one benefit of listening to God is liberation. "Listening makes us independent of illegitimate human influence," he writes, "it liberates us from worn-out orthodoxies and inherited prejudices, as well as from modern oppressions, circumstances, and ambitions—not to mention overwrought emotions." It could also liberate us from the dominant clichés of our society. "Listening to God instead of to the clamoring voices of our culture can free us from myriad personal fears and anxieties."

Klaus also believes that this discipline has a spin-off in a return to creativity and spontaneity. I remember on one of his visits to Oregon he told us, "Listening to God in a morning quiet time may be the only access to creativity for some of us who are not natural geniuses."

Klaus naturally approaches the subject as a Christian theologian. But I have found over the years, working among Jews, Hindus, Muslims, Buddhists, that the idea of seeking direction from a higher power can be a uniting bond between people of different faiths, and, indeed, even a gateway to faith for those in our own society who are turned off by the hypocrisy of those whose Christian language is not matched by Christian living. I have seen countless examples of deadlocked situations where the wisdom that is available in a time of quiet becomes the reference point for amicable solutions.

So, 40 years on, I'm still looking forward to what God might be wanting to tell me, and us, to do next. And to what God might be able to achieve in our community and the world through those who take the time to listen.

14 JUNE 1990